BILLY

the

KID

COOK BOOK

**A Fanciful Look at the Recipes and Folklore
from Billy the Kid Country**

by

Lynn Nusom

**GOLDEN
WEST ☼
PUBLISHERS**

Front cover art by Hugh Marshall

Other books by Lynn Nusom:
    Tequila Cook Book
    New Mexico Cook Book
    Christmas in New Mexico Cook Book
    Christmas in Arizona Cook Book

DEDICATION

This book is dedicated with heartfelt thanks to my wife, Guylyn Morris Nusom. Her assistance with all phases of the preparation of this book, including recipe creation, recipe testing, research, proofreading and finding historical materials–was invaluable.

Printed in the United States of America

3rd Printing © 2003

ISBN #1-885590-32-6

Golden West Publishers, Inc.
4113 N. Longview Ave.
Phoenix, AZ 85014, USA
(602) 265-4392

Visit our website: www.goldenwestpublishers.com

Table of Contents

(Continued next page)

Table of Contents

CHAPTER THREE

Mexican Dishes

CHAPTER FOUR

Cowboy Vittles

(Continued next page)

Table of Contents

CHAPTER FIVE

Ranch Life & the Lincoln

Vegetables & Side Dishes

(Continued next page)

Table of Contents

CHAPTER SIX
Doing Time in New Mexico 81

Desserts

EPILOGUE
The Story Ends, The Legend Begins 101

Beverages

INTRODUCTION

It's easy to see why Billy the Kid made New Mexico his stomping ground. Anyone who lives there or visits New Mexico will certainly tell you that it is indeed "The Land Of Enchantment." Not only is this a chamber of commerce slogan and the state motto, but most people living in New Mexico truly feel this way about their state and are fiercely loyal to New Mexico and its culture, including its colorful folklore.

The joke in the East used to be that if George Washington slept in every place attributed to him no wonder he was called the father of our country. This struck a familiar chord as I traveled throughout New Mexico and Arizona doing research for a book and it seemed that it was not the first president but Billy the Kid who was rumored to have either ate, slept or been in jail in practically every place I visited.

I was intrigued by all the stories surrounding the man and the places he was supposed to have been. The tales vary with the teller but the argument rages on, without resolution. Was Henry McCarty–aka William H. Bonney–aka Henry Antrim–aka Billy the Kid–a crook, hoodlum and murderer, or a loyal cowboy and freedom fighter?

Whatever he may have been, his name certainly lives on in the annals of southwestern folklore and graces the marquees of all kinds of businesses, including hotels, restaurants, bars, saloons, beauty shops, curio-shops and countless other enterprises.

This book is a sampling of some of the unique food prepared by the residents of the places Billy the Kid frequented. We will visit a few of the spots where the gunslinger left his mark and where he was said to have either passed through, lived in, worked

(Continued on next page)

in, or fought in. Although some of these locations and activities may be suspect to historians, it doesn't stop New Mexicans from having lively discussions about this controversial man who has spawned so many legends.

Although many of the exploits that generated these stories occurred in the southwest, Billy the Kid was actually born on New York City's lower east side.

The most likely scenario is that Billy was the illegitimate son of Catherine McCarty. Although the identity of his father is not really known, some historians believe the father's name was also McCarty–although he was not related to Catherine. Other sources list his mother as the Widow McCarty and assume that Billy was a legitimate son fathered by her first husband. Birth certificates were rare in the middle of the 19th century, although the hospitals of the time kept birth records. However, no paper trail has been found for Billy's debut into the world which would indicate that he was probably born at home in the predominately Irish fourth precinct of New York City.

His birthday has been reported to be either November 20th, or 23rd, 1859. Modern day astrologers have even done his horoscope based on both of these dates but in reading them I am inclined to think that their interpretation of his "stars" is based more on what they have read of his life than what they saw in the galaxy.

The McCarty/Bonney family left New York when little Henry/William/Billy was a very young boy. They lived for a short time in Kansas where some historians believe that Mrs. McCarty/Bonney married William H. Antrim. They then moved on to Santa Fe, New Mexico where other writers feel the two were married in 1873. But it wasn't until the family finally made their home in Silver City, New Mexico that Billy was old enough to start making the impressions that are now the stuff of legends.

CHAPTER ONE

BILLY THE KID'S
ADOLESCENCE
SILVER CITY, NEW MEXICO

After the Antrim's brief sojourn in Santa Fe (see *Introduction*) the family moved to Silver City and Billy's stepfather, William Antrim, began the task of looking for work. He had heard that fortunes were being made in the mines and it had always been his nature to look for a quick score. However, he didn't find the instant success he had hoped for. So, after a short period of time he was forced by the family's dwindling finances to settle for a job with a local butcher named Knight.

Billy was pressed into service to help his stepfather in the butcher shop. Mrs. Knight became very fond of the young man and he was often invited to the Knight ranch at Burro Mountain where he was treated like one of the family and, in turn, he helped out with the numerous chores. William Antrim soon tired of the regimented twelve-hour days in the butcher shop and quit in order to try his hand at prospecting again. However, Billy remained close friends with the Knight family and he and his brother boarded with them from time to time.

Billy went to school in Silver City, but the delights of hanging out with his buddies and watching the comings and goings of the miners and cowboys proved much more interesting.

Again, various books and oral histories differ on the beginnings of Billy's trouble in Silver City.

In one version he and one of his friends often tormented the local Chinese laundry man. One day when the laundry man was making a delivery, they broke into the back of the laundry and found the Chinese man's stash of gold coins. The man came back

(continued page 11)

in time to catch them in the act and Billy killed him. Rather than stay and face the consequences, he fled to Mexico. He was supposed to have stayed there several years before returning to New Mexico by way of El Paso del Norte. In this version, his mother died when he was in Mexico and he regretted not being there with her.

But another version has Billy and one of his friends stealing laundry from the Chinese laundry's line (in this version *two* Chinese men ran the laundry). The men caught the boys in the act and the sheriff threw them in jail where they stayed a few days, befriended the deputies and, when their attention was elsewhere, escaped.

Prior to this Billy had worked as a busboy for the owners of a local hotel. They had befriended him and he trusted them. Now he turned to them for a place to hide and soon after went to Arizona on a "borrowed horse" or hitched a ride with a man in a buckboard (depending on who was telling the story) and there he went to work on a ranch.

A third account of the first time Billy the Kid was in real trouble had him walking on the wooden sidewalks of Silver City with his mother when some drunken miners made derogatory comments about her. Billy reportedly got into a fist-fight with the older man responsible for the name calling. Billy came out the loser in the fight and harbored a resentment about it for several days. Finally he sought out the man in a saloon, killed him and then took off–to Arizona or Mexico–depending on who is spinning the yarn.

A common thread through all the stories is that Billy was very fond and protective of his mother and did not get along with his step-father. It is said that he later confided to friends that his mother had been the most stable and positive influence in his life and that her death at the age of thirty-four affected him deeply.

Escabèche

This is a delightful way to serve vegetables as an appetizer or first course. Vegetables such as carrots, cauliflower and zucchini are cooked with spices and then marinated with lime juice and hot chiles.

This is great served with crisp homemade tortilla chips and a cool drink or Mexican beer.

1 white onion, chopped
12 cloves garlic, sliced
4 carrots, thinly sliced on the diagonal
1/2 teaspoon coarsely ground black pepper
1 1/2 cups white vinegar
1/2 cup olive oil
2 cups water
2 tablespoons salt
1 head cauliflower, broken into flowerettes
6 bay leaves, broken in half
3 zucchini, sliced on the diagonal
1 teaspoon ground thyme
1 teaspoon ground oregano
1 teaspoon ground marjoram
1/2 cup lime juice
1 jicama, peeled and sliced
1/2 cup pickled jalapeños

Put all the ingredients, except lime juice, jicama and jalapeños, in a large nonreactive pot, bring to a boil then reduce the heat and simmer for 10 minutes. Let cool, then add the lime juice, jicama and jalapeños. Store, covered, in the refrigerator for up to 2 weeks. Remove bay leaves before serving.

Stuffed Jalapeños

These are great as hors d'oeuvres and make a perfect accompaniment to a large, frosty margarita. As jalapeños vary widely in amounts of "heat" it's always wise to sample a tiny bite before trying to eat a whole one.

12 jalapeños
Velveeta® cheese, cut into long fingers (slices),
    just smaller than the size of the jalapeños
1 cup cornmeal
1 cup all-purpose flour
2 teaspoons baking powder
1/2 teaspoon salt
1 cup milk
1 egg
1 teaspoon paprika
Dash of Tabasco®
Oil for deep frying

Cut off the stem end of jalapeños, scoop out the seeds (be sure and wear rubber gloves and wash your hands carefully. Do not rub your eyes or lips with your hands when handling chiles.) Stuff the cheese fingers in the jalapeños. Mix the rest of the ingredients (except oil) together to form a batter. Chill the batter in the refrigerator for an hour. Dip the stuffed jalapeños in the batter, chill in the refrigerator for an hour then deep fry until brown. The batter must be very cold to stick to the chiles.

Yields 1 dozen stuffed peppers.

Chile Shrimp Spread

1 can (5 oz.) peeled, deveined small shrimp, drained
1/2 cup butter, at room temperature
1/2 teaspoon Dijon mustard
2 dashes Tabasco® or to taste
1 clove garlic, minced
1 tablespoon lemon juice
1 jalapeño, seeded and diced

Mash the shrimp into the butter, then mix in the rest of the ingredients. Serve with party rye or crackers.

Meatballs Diablo

2 tablespoons bacon drippings or olive oil
1 medium onion, finely chopped
1 pound lean ground beef
1/2 pound ground pork
3 eggs
2 dashes of Tabasco® or to taste
1/2 cup dried bread crumbs
1/2 teaspoon ground cumin
1 clove garlic, minced
1/2 teaspoon ground nutmeg
1 tablespoon chopped fresh parsley
cooking oil

Heat the bacon drippings or oil in a frying pan, and cook the onion until soft. Mix together the ground beef and ground pork in a mixing bowl and stir in the onions. Lightly beat the eggs and add to the meat mixture. Stir in the Tabasco, bread crumbs, cumin, garlic, nutmeg, and parsley and form into balls approximately the size of walnuts. Fry the meatballs in the cooking oil over medium heat until well browned and done through. Place meatballs in **Red Chile Sauce** and serve with rice.

Yields 2 dozen meat balls.

Red Chile Sauce

2 tablespoons butter
2 tablespoons all-purpose flour
1 1/2 cups beef stock or broth
1/4 cup red wine
1 clove garlic, finely minced
1 teaspoon ground New Mexico red chile
1/2 teaspoon salt
1/2 teaspoon freshly ground black pepper

Melt the butter, stir in the flour and stir constantly letting the flour brown slightly. Slowly stir in the beef stock and wine. Stir until the sauce starts to thicken, then turn down the heat to simmer. Stir in the garlic, chile, salt and pepper. Let cook, over low heat, until just heated through.

Guacamole ¡Muy Sabroso!

(Savory Avocado Dip)

3 ripe avocados, peeled, pitted and mashed
4 teaspoons fresh lime juice
1/4 cup mayonnaise
1 red, ripe tomato, diced
1/4 red onion, diced
1/2 teaspoon freshly ground black pepper
1/2 teaspoon salt
1 teaspoon chopped fresh cilantro

Mix all the ingredients together and serve with **Chicken Fajitas** (page 51) or as an appetizer with tortilla chips.

Eggs Diablo

6 eggs, hard boiled, shelled and cut in half lengthwise
1 tablespoon mayonnaise
1 tablespoon sour cream
1/2 teaspoon garlic salt
1/4 teaspoon celery salt
1/2 teaspoon freshly ground black pepper
1 jalapeño, seeded and finely chopped
Black olives, sliced into rings
Paprika

Carefully remove the yolks from the whites of the eggs. Place the yolks in a bowl and mash them with a fork. Add the mayonnaise, sour cream, garlic powder, celery salt and black pepper and combine. Spoon the mixture into the egg white halves, garnish with jalapeños, black olive rings and a sprinkle of paprika.

Serves 4-6.

Navajo Fry Bread

This is an easy bread that can be made when unexpected visitors arrive. Billy the Kid had a lot of friends around the New Mexico Territory and one can imagine a ranch wife fixing this great-tasting bread after Billy rode up for a visit, or to hide out for a few days.

4 cups all-purpose flour
1 teaspoon baking powder
2 tablespoons lard*

1 1/2 cups lukewarm water
Peanut oil

Sift the flour and baking powder together in a mixing bowl. Cut the lard into the flour with a pastry cutter or fork. Add the water and knead into a workable dough. Leave the dough in the mixing bowl; cover with a towel and let stand for 20 minutes. Divide the dough into 12 equal size balls. Stretch and slap each ball to about 5 inches in diameter and poke a hole in the center. Heat the peanut oil to 375° and fry the breads, one at a time until golden brown.

Yields 12 pieces.

*I know that a lot of people try not to use lard in this day and age–but believe me I haven't found a substitute that will work as well for this recipe.

Cheese Puffs

2 cups all-purpose flour
1/2 pound butter
1/4 teaspoon salt
1/4 teaspoon cayenne

1/2 pound cheddar
   cheese, grated
1 egg, lightly beaten

Preheat oven to 425°. Cut the flour into the butter. Mix the salt, cayenne and cheese into the flour mixture and form into a ball. Roll out on a lightly floured board to 1/4-inch thickness. Using a small cutter, cut out 1 to 1 1/2-inch circles. Place on a lightly greased cookie sheet. Brush with the egg and bake for 10 to 12 minutes.

Buttermilk Biscuits

Biscuits were a popular staple in the Anglo diet during the mid-1800s. This recipe uses buttermilk which was plentiful and gives these biscuits a nice, rich texture. There is nothing better for breakfast than biscuits with butter and home-made preserves. Or, try them hot from the oven, with **New Mexico-Style Country Gravy** *(see page 64) spooned over them for an easy, filling breakfast.*

2 1/2 cups all-purpose flour
2 teaspoons baking powder
1/2 teaspoon baking soda
1/2 teaspoon salt
1/3 cup solid vegetable shortening
1 cup buttermilk
Melted butter

Sift the flour with the baking powder, baking soda and salt. Cut shortening into the dry ingredients with a pastry cutter until you have very fine pieces. Stir in the buttermilk with a fork and mix well. Place dough on a lightly floured pastry board, knead about 10 times and roll out to 1/2-inch thickness. Cut with a biscuit cutter that has been lightly floured (my grandmother used to use a drinking glass). Place the biscuits in 2 lightly greased 9-inch metal pie pans, brush the tops of the biscuits with melted butter and bake in a 450° oven for 10 minutes or until done.

Yields 16 biscuits.

THE GRANT COUNTY HERALD

Silver City, New Mexico   *Sunday, September 26, 1875*

Henry McCarty, who was arrested on Thursday and committed to jail to await the action of the grand jury, upon the charge of stealing clothes from Charley Sun and Sam Chung, celestials sans cue, sans Joss sticks, escaped from prison yesterday through the chimney. It is believed that Henry was simply the tool of 'Sombrero Jack' who done the actual stealing whilst Henry done the hiding. Jack has skipped out.

* * *

Plaza Corn Bread

2 cups yellow corn meal
2 teaspoons baking soda
1 teaspoon salt
2 cups milk
1 can (16 oz.) cream-style corn
1/2 cup melted butter
4 eggs, well beaten
1 medium onion, finely chopped
1 cup chopped cooked ham
1 jalapeño, seeded and chopped
1 cup grated Monterey Jack cheese

Preheat oven to 375°. Combine the cornmeal, salt and baking soda then add the milk, corn, butter and eggs. Stir in the chopped onions, ham, jalapeño and cheese. Pour batter into a lightly greased 9 x 13 baking pan and bake for 45 minutes. Serve with well-seasoned pinto beans and cole slaw.

Serves 4.

Beer Biscuits

This is a quick and easy biscuit recipe that uses a prepared biscuit mix. The beer gives the biscuits a unique, delightfully light flavor.

4 cups Bisquick®
1 tablespoon cooking oil
2 tablespoons sugar
1 can (12 oz.) beer at room temperature

Preheat oven to 400°. Mix all the ingredients together and pour into greased muffin tins. Fill only 1/2 full. Let sit about 20 minutes. Bake for 15 minutes or until the biscuits are nicely browned.

Yields 24 biscuits.

CHAPTER TWO

FLEEING THE LAW
INTO ARIZONA

Because Billy was slightly built he had no problem wiggling up the chimney of the Silver City jail and making an easy getaway. This was the first of many jailbreaks Billy was to pull off in the years to come.

No one knows for sure exactly what happened during the following two years after this first escape–but it seems likely that he "borrowed" a horse and road to western Arizona where he worked on various ranches. He soon became adept at tending to the horses, punching cows, riding, roping, and a hundred and one other ranch chores. This stay in Arizona was sure to most likely be the time he perfected his skill with guns.

He then drifted to Camp Grant and was said to have worked at a hotel owned by Miles Wood. It was there he fell in with a group of men, including John Mackie, who were engaged in various criminal activities including cattle rustling.

Mackie had been in trouble with the law over shooting a man in a card game and soon he and Billy had teamed up to steal horses and anything else that was easy pickings.

One of the horses they stole belonged to a cavalry sergeant who tracked Billy down. He retrieved the horse and let Billy walk back to town. Then he filed a complaint with the justice of the peace and an arrest warrant was issued for Henry Antrim (the Kid).

For a short time Billy eluded the constable trying to serve the warrant. However, one morning as the justice of the peace was having breakfast he saw Mackie and Billy coming into the

(Continued next page)

hotel dining room. The quick-witted justice changed places with the waiter and hid a gun under a tray. He went over to their table and instead of serving the pair a meal he arrested them. He promptly escorted them to the guardhouse on the post where they were to be held until they could be moved to a civilian jail.

Once again Billy slipped out of his cell and was on the lam. Later, probably in the summer of 1877, he showed up at Camp Grant again where he got into a fracas with a blacksmith working at the camp. The man was a known bully and repeatedly harassed Billy about all sorts of things, including his small stature.

They were both in the same saloon one day and the man started calling Billy names, most likely reflecting on his parentage. Billy took offense and they scuffled. Billy shot the blacksmith in the stomach and he died the next day.

The coroner's jury found the shooting unjustifiable and criminal which meant that Billy was to be held until a territorial grand jury was convened. However, Billy lost no time in leaving as he figured that back in New Mexico the authorities in Arizona wouldn't be able to touch him.

He rode to Burro Mountain, southwest of Silver City, and hid out at the Knight ranch there. However, after awhile he was afraid the Arizona authorities might still come for him so he decided he'd better leave. The Knights gave him a horse and he headed for the Mesilla Valley near Las Cruces, New Mexico.

Son-Of-A-Gun Stew

The combination of pork and beef makes a terrific tasting dish. In Billy's day this stew was cooked all day in a cast iron pot hanging from a hook in the back of a fireplace. I've brought this up-to-date and use a two step method; cooking the meat in a crockpot and then quickly finishing off the stew on top of the stove. I usually cook enough meat to not only make the stew but have some left over to make burritos or another dish.

Meat:
- 3 pounds chuck or other inexpensive beef roast
- 2 pounds pork roast or boneless pork ribs
- 2 bay leaves, broken in half
- 1 teaspoon dried parsley
- 2 cloves garlic, chopped
- 1 tablespoon dried, minced onion flakes
- 1 tablespoon Worcestershire sauce
- 1 tablespoon instant beef stock or 1 can beef broth
- Water

Vegetables:
- 2 tablespoons olive oil
- 1 medium yellow onion, chopped
- 1 green or red bell pepper, seeded and chopped
- 2 large carrots, chopped into small bite-size pieces
- 4 medium potatoes, peeled, cooked and cut into eighths
- 2 tablespoons butter
- 2 tablespoons all-purpose flour
- Juice from the cooked meat

Cut the meat into chunks small enough to fit in your crockpot. Place the bay leaves, parsley, garlic, onion flakes and Worcestershire on top of the meat. Mix the instant beef stock with a cup of hot water and pour over the meat, or use the beef broth and pour over the meat. Add enough water to cover the meat, cover and cook on high for 1 hour, reduce the heat to low and cook for 4-5 hours more or until the meat is tender.

Remove the meat from the crockpot. Divide the meat in half and cut one half of it into bite-size pieces. (Save the other half

(Continued on next page)

for another dish such as burritos.) Strain the juice from the crockpot and let cool. Skim off any excess fat and reserve the juice.

Heat the oil in a large Dutch oven or heavy pot, stir in the onion, bell pepper and carrots and cook over medium heat until the onion and bell pepper are tender. Remove the vegetables to a bowl. Melt the butter in the pot, stir in the flour and brown for a minute or so. Whisk in the strained juice from the meat until you have the consistency of light cream. Add water if you do not have enough juice or want it thinner.

Add the vegetables back to the pot. Then add the potatoes, meat and salt and pepper to taste.

Cook for 20 to 30 minutes over low heat until everything is warmed through and the flavors meld. Serve in large shallow bowls with sourdough or dark, crusty bread.

Serves 4-6

Cream of Avocado Soup

4 avocados, peeled, pitted and quartered
2 cups chicken stock or broth
1/2 white onion, chopped
1 teaspoon chopped fresh cilantro
1 jalapeño, seeded and chopped
1 tablespoon lemon juice
Approximately 6 cups half-and-half or milk
Chopped parsley for garnish

Put all ingredients except half and half and parsley in blender, and blend until smooth. Add enough half and half or milk to make the mixture the consistency of a cream soup. Pour into a saucepan and heat over low heat until warm. Garnish with chopped parsley and serve at once.

Serves 4.

Green Chile Stew

This is a popular New Mexico dish that is particularly good on a cold winter night and is excellent served with warm flour tortillas.

3 to 4 tablespoons olive oil
2 cloves garlic, minced
1 large yellow onion, chopped
1 pound lean beef, cut into bite-size pieces
1 pound lean pork, cut into bite-size pieces
1/4 cup all-purpose flour
1 1/2 cups beef stock or broth
6 cups water
6 green chiles, roasted, peeled, seeded and chopped
4 large potatoes, peeled and diced
1 teaspoon ground black pepper
1/2 teaspoon oregano
1 tablespoon finely chopped fresh parsley
1 teaspoon salt

Heat the oil in a large pot and sauté the garlic and onions for 4 to 5 minutes. Dredge the beef and pork in the flour and brown in the pan (add more oil, if necessary). Add the beef stock or broth and water and cook for 1 hour. Then add the rest of the ingredients and cook over low heat for approximately 1 hour or until meat and potatoes are done.

Serves 8-10.

Pecos Posole Soup

1 pound lean beef, cut into bite-size pieces
1 pound lean pork, cut into bite-size pieces
1 large yellow onion, chopped
4 cloves garlic, minced
1 teaspoon freshly ground black pepper
1 teaspoon salt
1 tablespoon chopped fresh parsley
1 teaspoon chopped fresh cilantro
1/2 teaspoon oregano
1 teaspoon ground cumin
1 red, ripe tomato, diced
4 cups chicken broth or stock
4 cups water
2 tablespoons red chile flakes
1 large can (6 lb. 10 oz.) white hominy

Sauté beef and pork with onion, garlic and seasonings in a large pot. Add the rest of the ingredients, except hominy, cover and simmer over low heat for one hour. Add hominy with the liquid from the can and continue cooking for 1 more hour, stirring occasionally over low heat. If necessary add more water.

Serves 6-8.

Tortilla Soup

The foundation of the cuisine in Mesilla has long been the spicy and wonderfully accented dishes that have a strong Mexican heritage. Tortilla soup brings some of these flavors from south of the border to your kitchen.

3 tablespoons olive oil
1 yellow onion, chopped
1 clove garlic, minced
1 cup peeled tomatoes
6 cups chicken stock or broth
1 tablespoon chopped cilantro
1/2 teaspoon salt
1/2 teaspoon freshly ground black pepper
2 cups tortilla chips (or corn tortillas fried in olive oil until crisp,
    cooled and broken into pieces)
1 jalapeño, seeded and diced
6 tablespoons grated Monterey Jack cheese

Sauté the garlic and onion in the olive oil until the onion is soft. Spoon the onion and garlic into a blender with the tomatoes, 1 cup of the chicken stock and the cilantro. Blend until smooth. Pour the mixture into a saucepan, stir in the rest of the chicken stock, salt and black pepper and cook over medium heat until hot.

Coarsely crumble the tortilla chips into the bottoms of individual soup bowls, pour the soup over the chips, sprinkle the diced jalapeño and the cheese over the top of the soup and serve at once.

Serves 6-8.

Crookneck Squash Soup

2 tablespoons olive oil
1/4 cup butter
1 large yellow onion, chopped
2 ribs celery, chopped
3 medium yellow crookneck squash, sliced
2 carrots, sliced
1 green bell pepper, chopped
2 sweet potatoes, peeled and cubed
2 white potatoes, peeled and cubed
2 mild green chiles, roasted, peeled, seeded and chopped
1 teaspoon freshly ground black pepper
1/4 teaspoon cayenne pepper
1 teaspoon salt
2 cups chicken broth or stock
6 cups water
Sprigs of cilantro

Heat oil and butter in a large soup pot and sauté onion, celery and squash for 5 to 6 minutes. Add the rest of the ingredients and cook, covered, for 1 hour. Garnish with sprigs of cilantro and serve.

Serves 6-8.

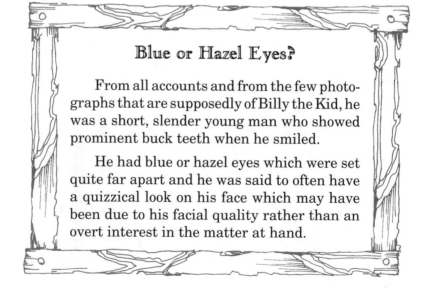

Blue or Hazel Eyes?

From all accounts and from the few photographs that are supposedly of Billy the Kid, he was a short, slender young man who showed prominent buck teeth when he smiled.

He had blue or hazel eyes which were set quite far apart and he was said to often have a quizzical look on his face which may have been due to his facial quality rather than an overt interest in the matter at hand.

Chile Cheese Soup

1 clove garlic, minced
1 onion, chopped
2 tablespoons butter
4 oz. cream cheese cut into cubes
2-3 green chiles, roasted, peeled, seeded and chopped
1 can (14 oz.) peeled tomatoes, chopped
1 can (5 oz.) low fat evaporated milk
1 can (14 1/2 oz.) chicken broth
2 teaspoons fresh lime juice
3-4 dashes Tabasco® sauce
1 teaspoon chopped fresh cilantro
Bacon bits
Tortilla chips

In a saucepan, cook the garlic and onion in butter over low heat until the onion is soft. Stir in the cream cheese over low heat and stir until the cheese is melted. Add chiles and tomatoes and cook over medium high heat, stirring occasionally, 8 to 10 minutes or until the liquid is evaporated. Add milk, chicken broth, lime juice, Tabasco, and cilantro. Cook over medium heat 8 to 10 minutes more, but do not let boil. Pour into serving bowls, sprinkle bacon bits over the top and serve with tortilla chips on the side.

Serves 4-6.

Photo courtesy of Southwest Studies

Caldo

The English translation for caldo is "broth". However, in many parts of the southwest caldo has now come to mean a clear soup with chunks of meat and vegetables.

1 to 2 cups of cooked meat* cut into bite-size pieces
4 potatoes, peeled and quartered
1 onion, quartered
2 carrots, peeled and sliced
2 turnips, peeled and quartered
1 head cabbage coarsely chopped
2 ears of fresh corn, sliced into 2-inch rounds
2 cups chicken stock or broth
6 cups water
1 teaspoon salt
1 teaspoon freshly ground black pepper
1 lime, quartered
1 tablespoon chopped fresh cilantro
2 jalapeños, seeded and diced
Cooked white rice

Place all the ingredients (except the lime, cilantro and jalapeños) in a large soup pot and simmer over medium heat for 1 hour. Ladle into large soup bowls and top with a sprinkling of cilantro and jalapeño. Serve with a wedge of lime and a bowl of hot rice on the side.

Serves 4-6.

*Chicken, roast beef or roast pork or a combination of all.

Cider Stew

3 tablespoons olive oil (In Billy's day cooks would have used
    bacon drippings)
2 medium yellow onions, chopped
3 tablespoons all-purpose flour
2 pounds lean stewing beef, cut into cubes
1/2 teaspoon ground black pepper
1/2 teaspoon ground sage
1 rib celery, chopped
1 tablespoon chopped fresh parsley
2 cups apple cider
2 cups water
1 tablespoon tomato sauce
3 large potatoes, peeled and cut into quarters
3 to 4 medium carrots, sliced

Heat oil in a large heavy pot and sauté onions until soft. Put flour in a paper sack or plastic bag and coat the pieces of meat with the flour. If needed, add more oil to the pot and then brown the meat. Add pepper, sage, celery, parsley, cider, water and tomato sauce and bring to a boil. Reduce heat and simmer for 1 hour. Add potatoes and carrots and cook for 45 minutes more or until meat and vegetables are tender.

Serves 6-8

Hacienda Stew

While roaming through the northern part of Mexico, Billy and his companion may have incurred the wrath of the monte dealers and other gamblers, but they won the hearts of several Mexicans, including the Doña (lady of the house) of a large hacienda who thought the "pobre gringos" (poor white men) needed some good food to fatten them up.

The following stew may be one of the dishes the Doña and her kitchen helpers made for the two visiting "Norte Americanos."

2 tablespoons olive oil
1 large yellow onion, chopped
4 cloves garlic, chopped
1/2 teaspoon ground cumin
1 teaspoon oregano
2 pounds lean beef, cut into cubes
2 tablespoons powdered red chile
1 tablespoon freshly ground black pepper
1 tablespoon chopped parsley or cilantro
1/4 cup red wine
6 cups water
3 potatoes, peeled, and cut into quarters
3 tomatoes, peeled and chopped
4 carrots, sliced

Heat olive oil in a heavy pan or Dutch oven. Sauté onion and garlic until onion is soft. Add cumin, oregano and beef and brown the beef on all sides. Stir in powdered chile, black pepper, parsley and wine. Add the water and simmer over low heat for one hour. Add potatoes, tomatoes and carrots and continue cooking until beef is tender and potatoes are done, approximately one more hour.

Serves 4-6.

Cowboy Cole Slaw

I'm not sure the cowboys during the 1800s were the romantic characters that novels and movies have made them out to be. They spent long days, weeks and even months out on the trail, without many conveniences. They did have to eat, however, and usually had a trail cook. Again, I'm not sure he was always the wise-cracking, grizzled old man shown in films. But one thing is certain, he either cooked well or he was history! This cole slaw could have been served on the trail–although I doubt it. However it will be great for the cowboys, and cowgirls around YOUR chuck wagon.

1 large head cabbage, finely shredded
1 large yellow onion, finely chopped
1 green bell pepper, seeded and chopped
1 red bell pepper, seeded and chopped
1/2 cup chopped dill pickle

Place the shredded cabbage in a mixing bowl with the onion, bell peppers, and pickles. Mix well with the following **Cowboy Dressing** and chill in the refrigerator for one hour before serving.

Serves 6-8.

Cowboy Dressing

1 cup mayonnaise
1 teaspoon dried parsley
1 green onion, finely chopped
    (include green tops)
1/2 teaspoon powdered New Mexico
    red chile
1/2 teaspoon freshly ground
    black pepper
Juice of 1 lemon
1 teaspoon Dijon mustard

Mix all the ingredients together and use to dress **Cowboy Cole Slaw.**

Fiesta Salad

One can imagine Billy in a small Mexican town waiting for some action–like a monte game. He strolls through the dusty streets and then comes across a group of children in the garden of a small house. They are noisily cheering on a blindfolded child armed with a stick who is attacking and missing a brightly painted olla, or piñata.

It is a typical birthday celebration of the day. The olla, or piñata, is filled with sweets and goodies and the children take turns trying to break open the ceramic bowl swinging from a tree branch. The Kid leans against an adobe building, watching the little ones frolic, thinking about his own wandering childhood.

Suddenly the child wielding the stick breaks the olla and candies spill out and onto the ground. With shrieks of delight the rest of the children scramble around in the dirt for their share. Then the children's mothers and aunts summon them to a table laid under a cottonwood tree for a fiesta lunch, which might have included this salad.

4 oranges, peeled, seeded, and sectioned
2 bananas, peeled and sliced
1 small jicama, peeled and cut into bite-size pieces
2 tart apples, peeled, cored and cut into bite-size pieces
1 red bell pepper, seeded and chopped
juice of 1 pink grapefruit
1 cup coarsely chopped unsalted cashews
Shredded lettuce

Combine the oranges, bananas, jicama, apples, and bell peppers in a salad bowl. Pour grapefruit juice over the fruit, add cashews and lightly toss the salad.

Arrange the shredded lettuce on a serving plate or platter, spoon the fruit mixture on top of the lettuce and serve with **Fiesta Salad Dressing** (see next page)

Serves 6-8.

Fiesta Salad *(continued from previous page)*

Fiesta Salad Dressing

3 tablespoons grenadine
2 tablespoons white wine vinegar
1/2 cup mayonnaise
1/4 cup light cream
1 tablespoon poppy seeds

Mix all the ingredients together and serve on the side with *Fiesta Salad* (see previous page).

Cantaloupe Salad

1 large ripe cantaloupe, peeled, seeded and cut
    into bite-size pieces
2 cups seedless green grapes
1 cup mayonnaise
1 tablespoon chopped fresh mint leaves
1/3 cup fresh orange juice
2 tablespoons orange-flavored liqueur
Whole mint leaves

Place the cantaloupe and grapes in a salad bowl. In a small bowl mix together the mayonnaise, mint leaves, orange juice and orange liqueur until smooth. Pour over the fruit and toss lightly. Chill for an hour in the refrigerator, garnish with whole mint leaves and serve.

Serves 4-6.

Ranch-Style Potato Salad

6 large cooked potatoes, coarsely diced
2 celery ribs, chopped
2 to 3 dill pickles, chopped
6 tablespoons mayonnaise
1 tablespoon Dijon mustard
3 hard boiled eggs, diced
1 red onion, chopped
1/2 cup green salad olives, chopped
1/2 teaspoon salt
1 teaspoon freshly ground black pepper
1/2 teaspoon paprika
1 tablespoon finely chopped fresh parsley

Place all the ingredients except the paprika and parsley in a salad bowl and lightly toss. Cover and store in refrigerator until ready to serve. When ready to serve sprinkle the paprika and parsley over the top.

Serves 6-8.

Spanish Cucumber Salad

3 medium cucumbers, peeled and sliced
2 red, ripe tomatoes, quartered
1 medium red onion, sliced
1/2 cup sliced black olives
8 fresh basil leaves, chopped
3 tablespoons olive oil
1 tablespoon white vinegar
1 tablespoon dry sherry
1/2 teaspoon Dijon mustard
1/2 teaspoon ground white pepper
1/2 teaspoon salt

Combine the cucumbers, tomatoes, onions and olives in a salad bowl. Mix together the rest of the ingredients until smooth. Pour over the vegetables, toss lightly and serve.

Serves 6-8.

Green Pea Salad

1 package frozen green peas, thawed
2 ribs celery, chopped
2 sweet pickles, chopped
2 tart red apples, cored but unpeeled, chopped
1 tablespoon lemon juice
1/2 teaspoon salt
1 cup pecans, chopped
6 tablespoons mayonnaise
Lettuce leaves
Pecan halves

Mix all the ingredients together, except the lettuce and the pecan halves. Spoon the salad onto a bed of lettuce leaves, garnish with pecan halves and serve.

Serves 4.

The Legend of Billy the Kid

A horde of writers have tried to sort out the legend of Billy the Kid. It has not been an easy job, especially since even the newspapers almost a century closer to the facts did not agree on what transpired. The following is one version of what sent the Kid into a life of crime and on the run from the law.

EL PASO HERALD

El Paso, Texas   *August 29, 1901*

"There is a legend of home and mother connected with the earlier stages of the saga of Billy the Kid, perhaps the most thoroughly bad of all the bad men ever known in the really bad times of the West. History has it, with what accuracy let us not inquire too closely, that when Billy the Kid was yet a boy, not more than fourteen years of age, someone addressed to his mother a disrespectful remark. This was in Arizona, and at the time when resentments were swift and deadly. The story goes that the boy drew a knife, fatally stabbed the man and then fled from the country. From that time Billy the Kid became an outlaw, and an outlaw he remained for the seven years which completed the span of his short life."

Mexican Cauliflower Salad

1 large cauliflower, broken into flowerettes
1 medium red onion, sliced into rings
3 ripe tomatoes, cut into wedges
2 cucumbers, peeled and sliced
1 cup ripe black olives

Lightly toss the ingredients together in a salad bowl and dress with *Mexican Cauliflower Salad Dressing.*

Serves 6-8.

Mexican Cauliflower Salad Dressing

2 avocados, peeled, pitted and mashed
2 tablespoons lime or lemon juice
1/4 cup mayonnaise
1 tablespoon tequila
2 dashes Tabasco®
1/2 teaspoon salt
1/2 teaspoon freshly ground black pepper

Mix all the ingredients together to make a smooth dressing, pour over Mexican Cauliflower Salad, toss lightly and serve.

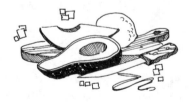

CHAPTER THREE

BILLY
IN
MEXICO?

Several writers, including Pat Garrett, have said that during the two years Billy the Kid was out of New Mexico, supposedly in Arizona, he also spent some time in Mexico.

It has been often reported that Billy had an affinity for Mexican people. It was also thought that he easily learned to speak fluent Spanish while he was in Arizona.

It is also likely that while he was in Arizona he joined forces with a man named Segura and that they drifted south of Tucson into Sonora and supported themselves by gambling. One tale from this time has it that a man named Martinez, an expert monte dealer, was openly hostile to Billy and often refused to pay him the full amount of money he won at the tables.

One afternoon Billy and Segura saddled up their horses and while Segura waited in the plaza, Billy went into the house where Martinez was dealing monte. As usual Martinez began insulting Billy, calling him a "gringo," along with more unprintable gibes. An exchange of insults between the two followed and it is possible that, among other things, Billy called the man a coward.

This infuriated Martinez and he drew a gun from under the gaming table, but Billy was too fast for him and shot him in the head. Martinez's bullet may have nicked Billy in the ear.

Billy beat a quick retreat from the gambling house and, with a posse of Mexicans on their heels he and Segura rode out of town. They eluded their pursuers and then headed to Chihuahua City.

There, Lady Luck deserted them when they tried to earn their keep by playing cards. One evening, however, Billy had won quite

(Continued on next page)

a bit of money playing monte when the dealer suddenly closed the game and told him that he didn't have the funds on hand to pay Billy what he owed him.

But the sharp-eyed Kid had seen the dealer put enough gold in his saddlebags to pay him. However, he didn't say anything about it to the man and got up and left. The dealer's double dealing that evening seems to be the reason that the man never made it home after the game and the gold in question disappeared.

Although Billy and his companion didn't appear in the gambling houses after that incident there were rumors that other card dealers were held up on their way home after a successful night of card playing.

Not long after, Segura and Billy made their way back north paying their way enroute with Spanish gold, which only added to the rumors concerning the duo's whereabouts and enterprises in Mexico.

If the two men were indeed in Chihuahua City they would most likely have come back north by way of El Paso.

People living in El Paso and San Elizario at the time later told anyone who would listen that the men spent time there and paid their bills with Spanish gold.

So it seems likely, given the time frame, that Billy the Kid might have been in Sonora before his run-in with the blacksmith at Camp Grant. Although it is not quite as feasible that he was also in Chihuahua and Texas at this time, it makes a good story.

Huevos Rancheros
(Ranch Style Eggs)

When Billy the Kid was growing up in Silver City there weren't any cornflakes or Fruit Loops® to start off the morning. The family undoubtedly raised chickens, so they had plenty of eggs and although meat and eggs served with biscuits was standard breakfast fare it is likely that after they moved west Billy's mother also quickly learned to prepare some tasty egg dishes from her neighbors of Mexican descent.

Vegetable oil
8 corn tortillas
8 eggs
4 tablespoons grated longhorn
  or colby cheese

Shredded lettuce
1 large red, ripe tomato,
  finely chopped
Refried Beans

Heat the oil in a frying pan, and dip the tortillas, one at a time, with tongs, in the hot oil until they are limp. Quickly drain on paper towels. Place two tortillas on each plate. Fry the eggs sunny side up (or to your taste) and place them on top of the tortillas. Top with the **Red Chile & Chorizo Sauce.** Sprinkle with cheese and place under the broiler until the cheese melts. Garnish with lettuce and tomato and serve with refried beans on the side.

Red Chile & Chorizo Sauce

2 tablespoons butter
2 tablespoons chopped white onion
1 clove garlic, minced
1/2 teaspoon ground cumin
1/2 teaspoon oregano
1 tablespoon powdered red chile
1/2 cup water
1 cup tomato sauce
1/2 teaspoon salt
1/2 teaspoon ground black pepper
1 tablespoon chopped fresh cilantro
1/2 pound chorizo or pork sausage, fried and crumbled

Melt butter in a frying pan, and cook the onions until they are translucent. Add the balance of ingredients. Stir and simmer for 10 to 15 minutes or until nicely blended.

Indian Taco

1 onion, chopped
1 clove garlic, minced
1 teaspoon chopped fresh parsley
3 tablespoons olive oil
1 pound ground beef
1 teaspoon red chile flakes
2 mild green chiles, roasted, peeled, seeded and chopped
Shredded lettuce
2 red, ripe tomatoes, chopped
Grated cheddar or longhorn cheese
Navajo Fry Bread (see p. 16)

Sauté the onion, garlic and parsley in the olive oil for 3-4 minutes, then add the ground beef, red chile flakes and green chile Cook, stirring with a fork, until the meat is brown and crumbled. Spoon some of the meat into the center of a piece of **Navajo Fry Bread,** top with shredded lettuce, chopped tomatoes and cheese. Serve with your favorite salsa.

Serves 4-6.

Breakfast Burrito

2 eggs
splash water
2 teaspoons butter
2 green onions, chopped
2 tablespoons diced cooked ham
1 jalapeño, seeded and chopped
2 flour tortillas
Grated cheddar or longhorn cheese

Lightly beat the eggs, add the water and beat again. Melt butter in a frying pan, stir in onion, ham and jalapeño. Pour the eggs over the mixture and cook over low heat until bottom is set, turn over and continue to cook until other side is done. Remove, divide in half and place each half on a warm flour tortilla, roll up, sprinkle with grated cheese and serve with refried beans.

Serves 2.

Cabbage, Corned Beef & Chile Hash

Cabbage and potatoes grew easily in Billy the Kid country and, before refrigeration, would keep in a cool cellar or shed for a long time without spoiling. The green chile gives this dish that little something extra. This is a comfort food at its best! Thank goodness hash is back!

3 tablespoons olive oil
1 medium yellow onion, finely chopped
4 medium potatoes, peeled, cooked and chopped
1 head of cabbage, cored and shredded
2 cups finely chopped corned beef (see p. 57)
2 green chiles, roasted, peeled, seeded and chopped
1/2 teaspoon salt
1 teaspoon ground black pepper
1/2 teaspoon cumin
1 teaspoon chopped cilantro

Pour the olive oil in a large pot, and sauté the onion until soft. Add the rest of the ingredients and cook, over low heat, until warmed through. Great served with warm flour tortillas.

Serves 4-6.

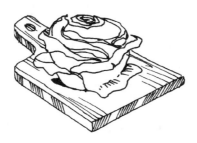

Steak Topped with Chile Con Queso

4 boneless rib-eye steaks, (6-8 oz. each)

Chile-Cheese sauce:
   1/2 cup cubed Velveeta® cheese
   1/3 cup low fat evaporated milk
   1 jalapeño, seeded and chopped
   1 clove garlic, minced
   1/4 teaspoon freshly ground black pepper
   Jalapeño slices

Broil the steaks to your taste. While they are cooking, melt the cheese in a saucepan or microwave, stir in milk until smooth. Add the jalapeño, garlic, and black pepper and stir again until thoroughly mixed. Place steaks on warm plates and spoon the chile-cheese sauce over the steaks, top with jalapeño slices and serve.

Serves 4.

Silver City Chorizo

1/2 pound ground round steak
1/2 pound ground pork
2 cloves garlic, minced
1/2 small yellow onion, finely chopped
2 tablespoons ground red chile
1 1/2 tablespoons white vinegar
1/2 teaspoon ground cumin
1/2 teaspoon ground sage
1/2 teaspoon ground oregano
1/2 teaspoon salt
1/2 teaspoon freshly ground black pepper

Mix all of the ingredients together, place in a glass bowl, cover with plastic wrap and place in the refrigerator overnight. Use in the *Rice, English Peas and Chorizo* (see p. 71) recipe or fry as you would any sausage and serve with scrambled eggs.

Billy's Beef Burrito

2 tablespoons olive oil
1 medium yellow onion, chopped
1 pound lean ground beef
1 clove garlic, minced
1/2 teaspoon ground cumin
1/2 teaspoon freshly ground black pepper
1/2 teaspoon salt
1 potato, peeled, cooked and diced
2 New Mexico green chiles, roasted, peeled, seeded
    and chopped
4-8 flour tortillas
Shredded lettuce
Sour cream
Salsa

Heat oil in a frying pan, then sauté onion for 3-4 minutes. Add ground beef, garlic, cumin, pepper and salt. Cook, stirring with a fork, until brown. Stir in the potato and green chiles and continue cooking until the potato and chiles are warmed through.

In a nonstick frying pan, heat each tortilla until just warm. Remove from pan, spoon a little of the beef mixture into center of each tortilla and roll up. Top with shredded lettuce, a tablespoon of sour cream and/or your favorite salsa. Serve with refried beans on the side.

Serves 4-8.

A Burro's Tale

One can imagine Billy and his compatriots of the time sitting around a campfire enjoying some *burritos* a lovely senorita had made for them in the town they had just ridden through.

One of the men wonders out loud how the Mexican people thought of putting meat, potatoes, chile and the like on a tortilla, rolling it and up and coming up with the *burrito*.

One of the cowboys, given to spinning yarns, comes up with the following story:

"In the old days there was this beautiful Indian girl who married a proud, hard-working Spanish boy. He was one of those kids who left the Spanish army when it marched up the Pecos.

In order to grow enough food to feed his new family the boy had to walk quite a distance from their home each day to find some land that was tillable. It was too far for him to come home to eat at noon-time. He loved the chile, beans and tortillas that his bride cooked for his lunch, but it was too far to carry pots of beans to the fields.

His clever young wife found a way that he could have the food he liked that would also be easy to carry. She mixed the beans and chile together and then spooned them onto a tortilla and rolled it up.

When he started bringing this innovative way to carry his lunch to work every day, the other men who walked with him or worked in the nearby fields would ask what he had.

'Oh,' he said, 'this is how my wonderful bride feeds me my favorite food. She gives me beans and chile and makes the tortilla carry it like a burro.'

And that's how *burritos* got their name."

Green Tomato Salsa

1 yellow onion, finely chopped
2 cloves garlic, minced
6-8 medium green tomatoes, chopped
2 red, ripe tomatoes, chopped
2 jalapeños, seeded and chopped
1 tablespoon chopped cilantro
1/2 teaspoon salt
3-4 dashes Tabasco® sauce
juice of one lime

Mix all the ingredients together in a nonreactive bowl, cover and chill in the refrigerator until ready to serve. Great as a topping for bean burritos or tacos. Or serve as a dip with tortilla chips.

Yields approximately 2 cups.

Tortas
(Mexican Sandwiches)

6 large bolillos (Mexican rolls), or substitute French baguettes
    (cut into thirds)
Butter
1 ripe avocado, peeled, pitted and mashed
1 clove garlic, minced
2 teaspoons lime juice
6 thick slices bacon, fried until crisp
6 slices Asadero or Monterey Jack cheese
Shredded lettuce
Sliced jalapeños

Split the rolls lengthwise. Spread cut sides of rolls with butter and toast on top of the stove in a cast iron skillet until lightly browned. Blend the avocado, garlic and lime juice together and spread on one half of each roll. Top with a slice of bacon, a slice of cheese, a sprinkle of shredded lettuce, and slices of jalapeño. Cover with other half of the roll and serve.

Serves 6.

Chile Chicken Over Rice

1 (3-3 1/2 pound) chicken
2 tablespoons coarse (kosher) salt
Water
8 to 10 cloves
1 medium onion
2 bay leaves

Soak the chicken in water with 2 tablespoons coarse (kosher) salt for 1/2 hour. Rinse under cold water then put into a large pot. Add water to the pot to cover the chicken. Stick the cloves in the onion and add it to the pot along with the bay leaves. Simmer the chicken over medium heat for 1 hour or until the meat falls off the bones. Let cool, remove the chicken meat from the bones, cut into bite-size pieces, and set aside. Skim off the fat, strain the broth and reserve.

3 tablespoons butter
3 tablespoons all-purpose flour
1 cup milk
1 cup reserved chicken broth
1 tablespoon red chile flakes
1 clove garlic, minced
1/2 teaspoon oregano
1/2 teaspoon dried sweet basil
Cooked rice
1/2 cup ripe black olives, sliced
Parsley

Melt the butter in a saucepan, stir in the flour to make a roux, add the milk and chicken broth and beat with a wire whisk until smooth. Stir in the red chile flakes, garlic, oregano and basil and cook, beating, until smooth. Add the chicken meat and continue to cook until hot, adding more of the chicken broth, if necessary. Serve hot over rice, garnish with the black olives and parsley. Serves 4.

Tri-Color Salsa

1 large red bell pepper, seeded and chopped
1 large green bell pepper, seeded and chopped
1 large yellow bell pepper, seeded and chopped
2 cups peeled and diced red, ripe tomatoes
1 onion, chopped
1/2 teaspoon salt
1/2 teaspoon freshly ground black pepper
1 tablespoon chopped cilantro
juice of 1 lemon

Mix all the ingredients together, cover and chill in the refrigerator until ready to serve. Excellent served as a condiment with roast meat, fajitas or as a dip with blue corn tortilla chips.

Yields approximately 2 cups.

Cilantro Salsa

This unique herb found its way into the early cooking of New Mexico by way of Mexico where it was introduced by the Spanish settlers. In Billy the Kid's day cilantro and coriander, the seed of the cilantro, were used in making such diversified things as sausages, candies called "comfits" and liqueurs. In today's cooking this delightful herb gives a distinctive taste to marinades, chile dishes, pot roasts, and stews.

4-5 roma tomatoes, peeled and chopped
3 tomatillos, peeled and chopped
1 small yellow onion, finely chopped
1 jalapeño, seeded and chopped
2 cloves garlic, minced
3 tablespoons white vinegar
1 tablespoon chopped fresh cilantro
1/2 teaspoon freshly ground black pepper
1/4 teaspoon oregano

Mix all the ingredients together. Chill in the refrigerator for at least an hour before serving.

Yields approximately 3 cups.

Just a Little Fun

The saloon doors swung open wide . . .
And in walked the Kid with ease
Just to have a little fun inside,
Play some cards–shoot the breeze.

A bar girl stepped onto the stage
And sang about her broken heart.
At Billy's table the ace was played,
Two men folded, figuring it was smart.

A man swaggered up through the smoky haze,
To pick a fight then and there.
He fixed Billy with the meanest gaze,
The Kid laughed it off without a care.

Next morning outside o'town,
They found him stone cold dead.
"Seeing him lying in the mud face down
Was a shame", the men said.

Somebody ordered up a bottle of rye
One man shook his head and said with a grin,
"What a way to die
It's sure to be a sin."

Then one old geezer blurted out
"It was the Kid that done him in
There ain't no doubt,
Going up against the Kid you can't win.

"Well, old Pat Garrett a'be on his trail,"
A player with a pair o'jacks said with hope,
"One of these days he's gonna wind up in jail
Or dangle from the end of a rope."

Then suddenly through those swinging doors
        with a lurch,
Came a laughing Billy twirling his gun
And the place was suddenly quiet as a church
Till they realized all the Kid wanted was
        just a little fun.

Tostadas

2 tablespoons olive oil
1 onion, chopped
1 clove garlic, finely minced
1 pound lean ground beef
1/2 teaspoon red chile flakes
1/4 teaspoon ground cumin
1/2 teaspoon salt
1/2 teaspoon freshly ground black pepper
1 1/2 cups cooked pinto beans
1 dozen corn tortillas
3 tablespoons cooking oil
Grated cheddar or longhorn cheese
Shredded lettuce
2 fresh tomatoes, chopped

Sauté the onion and garlic in the oil, add the meat and cook until lightly browned. Add the chile flakes, cumin, salt, pepper and beans and cook over medium heat until blended. While this is cooking, fry tortillas in the cooking oil until they are firm. Spoon meat and bean mixture on each of the tortillas. Sprinkle grated cheese on top of the meat, sprinkle shredded lettuce and chopped tomatoes on top of the cheese and serve with your favorite salsa.

Serves 6.

Pat Garrett
Photo courtesy New Mexico State Records Center and Archives

Pollo Picante

(Spicy Chicken)

1 cup all-purpose flour
6 chicken legs with thighs attached
3-4 tablespoons olive oil
1 red onion, sliced
2 jalapeños, seeded and diced
1 red bell pepper, sliced
1 1/2 cups sour cream
1 cup milk
1 teaspoon salt
1/4 teaspoon ground black pepper
1/4 teaspoon cayenne
2 cloves garlic

Preheat oven to 350°. Put flour in a paper sack or plastic bag. Shake the chicken pieces one at a time in the bag until coated with flour. Heat oil in a large frying pan and brown the chicken on all sides. Remove from the pan and arrange in a shallow 3 to 4-quart baking dish.

Top with sliced onion, jalapeños, and red pepper. Blend the sour cream, milk, salt, pepper, cayenne and garlic in a blender until smooth and pour over the chicken. Bake, uncovered, for 45 minutes to 1 hour or until the chicken is fork tender. Serve with rice or noodles.

Serves 6.

Chicken Fajitas

4 boneless, skinless chicken breasts
2 tablespoons coarse (kosher) salt
Cold water

Soak the chicken breasts in salt and cold water to cover for 30 minutes then drain and rinse under cold running water.

Marinade:
  Juice of 3 limes
  1/2 cup tequila
  2 tablespoons olive oil
  1/2 teaspoon ground New Mexico red chile
  1/2 teaspoon oregano
  1/2 teaspoon ground cumin
  1 teaspoon chopped fresh cilantro

Mix all the ingredients together and marinate the chicken breasts in the mixture for 2 hours in the refrigerator. Remove from the marinade, slice the chicken breasts into strips and grill over hot coals. Serve with grilled or sautéed onions, ***Guacamole ¡Muy Sabroso!*** (see page 15), sour cream, ***Pico de Gallo*** and warm tortillas.

Serves 4.

Pico de Gallo

(Spanish for "rooster's beak" Pico de Gallo is a relish made of finely chopped ingredients.)

1 medium yellow onion, finely chopped
2 cloves garlic, minced
2 red, ripe tomatoes, diced
3 jalapeños, seeded and chopped, or to your taste
1 tablespoon chopped fresh cilantro
Juice of 2 limes
2 teaspoons olive oil

Mix the onion, garlic, tomatoes and jalapeños together in a glass bowl. Stir in the cilantro, lime juice and oil. Cover and refrigerate 1 hour before serving. This is best eaten the day it's prepared as it does not store well.

Chile-Cheese Frittata

3 tablespoons butter
1/2 yellow onion, finely chopped
8 eggs, lightly beaten
1 teaspoon Worcestershire sauce
Several dashes of Tabasco® sauce, to your taste
1 clove garlic, minced
1 green chile, roasted, peeled, seeded and chopped
1 large potato, peeled, cooked and diced
1 large red, ripe tomato, peeled and diced
1/2 cup shredded Monterey Jack cheese
1/2 cup grated cheddar cheese

Melt the butter in a large nonstick frying pan and sauté the onion until limp. Lightly beat the eggs in a small bowl, then stir in the Worcestershire, Tabasco, and garlic. If needed, add more butter to the pan. Pour the eggs over the onions. Sprinkle the chile, potatoes, tomato, and both cheeses over the top of the eggs and cook, covered, about 15 minutes or until the eggs are set and the cheeses have melted.

Serves 4-6.

Chiles Rellenos Casserole

8-10 whole long green chiles,
    roasted, peeled and seeded
2 cups shredded Monterey
    Jack cheese
2 eggs
2 cups milk
1/2 cup all-purpose flour
1 teaspoon salt
1/2 teaspoon ground cumin
1/2 teaspoon oregano

Preheat oven to 350°. In the bottom of a buttered casserole dish, arrange the chiles. Sprinkle cheese on top. Lightly beat eggs then beat in flour, milk, salt, cumin and oregano until smooth. Pour over cheese and bake for 45 to 50 minutes or until set and lightly browned.

Serves 4-6.

CHAPTER FOUR

BILLY'S ESCAPADES IN MESILLA, NEW MEXICO

Mesilla, New Mexico was one of Billy the Kid's favorite haunts. Although a sleepy village now, with elegant, shuttered adobe homes, shops and restaurants geared to tourists–during Billy's day it was one of the largest towns in the New Mexico territory. It was the horse-changing and supply stopover for the famous Butterfield Overland Mail Stage. One could also make stagecoach connections in Mesilla and go south to Chihuahua or north to Santa Fe.

Low-slung adobe houses and business buildings lined the town's narrow, dusty streets. In addition to the stage stop and private homes, Mesilla had mercantile establishments, the Mesilla Hotel, bars and dance halls. Mesilla was the sort of rip-snorting, fun-loving town of which legends were spun and movies are made.

If you lived in the New Mexico Territory in the 1870s and 1880s this is the spot you headed for if you wanted to kick up your heels. Mesilla offered a plethora of bars and dance halls

(Continued on next page)

where dances were held almost nightly. There were also cockfights, bullfights and just plain fights. Very few men appeared in public without a gun or two and disputes were settled swiftly and effectively with these six-shooters.

It was indeed the wild west–an era when saloon keepers put up signs that read, "Don't shoot the musicians, they are doing the best they can." People traveled from as far away as Tucson, Santa Fe, and Chihuahua just to see what was happening and join the party.

Although the two were mutually exclusive–the year of the Kid's death in 1881 marked the beginning of the end for Mesilla. The railroad line going east and west decided that instead of laying track through Mesilla they would go just northeast of Mesilla through Las Cruces, now the second largest city in New Mexico–but then a small town dozing in the hot southwestern sun, much like Mesilla does today.

The following year the Doña Ana County seat was moved from Mesilla to Las Cruces and the village slumbered quietly until the 1980s when it was rediscovered by entrepreneurs and tourists looking for a taste of the Old West.

Tyrone Steak

Although the area around Silver City and Tyrone was known for its mining, ranching was also important to the region. On the ranch–steak was often just cooked in a little lard in a cast iron skillet. Here is a different, easy and very tasty way to prepare a cut of meat that might not be tender enough just grilled or broiled.

**1 boneless round steak (2 to 2 1/2 pounds and
    about 1 inch thick)**
4 tablespoons all-purpose flour
2 teaspoons ground red chile, divided
1 teaspoon ground black pepper
3 tablespoons cooking oil
1 large onion, peeled and chopped
1 clove garlic, finely chopped
1 cup crushed tomatoes
1 tablespoon vinegar
Water

Mix flour with 1 teaspoon of the ground chile and the black pepper. Dredge steak in the flour mixture. Heat the oil in a heavy skillet or Dutch oven (cast iron works best) and sauté the chopped onion and garlic until onions are soft. Add steak to the pan and sear on both sides. Add tomatoes, vinegar, the remaining ground chile and enough water to cover the meat. Cover the pan, reduce heat and cook over low heat for 1 1/2 hours or until the meat is tender.

Serves 4-6.

Traditional Boiled Beef

For a young boy growing up in Silver City there was nothing more intriguing than the Apache Indians who lived in the mountains. Billy and his friend, Jesse Evans, often practiced riding in the mountains, pretending to stalk the Indians. They also studied the Apache fighting tactics, and how the Indians lived. This education would serve Billy well later, during his travels in the desolate New Mexico Territory, and his encounters with both Indians and the law. After a day of youthful investigation of the area, one can imagine the ravenous appetites these boys had. Perhaps Mrs. Antrim served them a boiled beef dinner which was a popular and easy way to fix meat in the 1800s.

3 pounds lean beef roast
3 tablespoons olive oil
2 medium carrots, peeled and diced
2 ribs celery, diced
1 medium yellow or white onion, peeled and finely chopped
1 small white turnip, peeled and diced
2 bay leaves, broken in half
1 teaspoon ground black pepper
1 tablespoon paprika
1 tablespoon Worcestershire sauce
1 cup crushed tomatoes
2 tablespoons chopped fresh parsley
3 quarts boiling water

Wash and pat the beef dry. Pour the oil in a large pot or Dutch oven and sear the beef on all sides. Add the rest of the ingredients. Cook, covered, over medium heat for 2 1/2 to 3 hours or until the meat is tender. Remove meat, and let stand. Strain off vegetables and reserve the liquid. Make a roux of 2 tablespoons butter and 2 tablespoons all-purpose flour and add the strained stock to make a gravy to accompany the beef. Or let the stock cool, refrigerate and use as a soup stock. Slice the beef and serve with boiled new potatoes, fresh turnips and baby carrots.

Serves 6-8.

Corned Beef

Before refrigeration, one of the best ways of preserving meat was to "corn it." After the meat is cured it is great served all sorts of ways—corned beef and cabbage, mile-high sandwiches with sauerkraut and Swiss cheese, and corned beef hash.

1 (8 to 10 pound) beef brisket

Brine:
> **1/2 cup coarse (kosher) salt**
> **1 tablespoon sugar**
> **1 lemon, cut in half**
> **24 black peppercorns**
> **1 teaspoon saltpeter (available in drug stores)**
> **1/2 cup white vinegar**
> **3 bay leaves**
> **1 tablespoon parsley flakes**
> **1 quart water**

1/2 cup chopped celery leaves

Put all the ingredients, except the meat and celery leaves, in a non-aluminum saucepan and bring to a boil. Trim the fat off the meat and place it in a crock or large, heavy nonreactive pottery or glass bowl. Pour the hot mixture over the meat. Cover and let sit in the refrigerator for at least a week to ten days. When ready to cook, remove the meat from the brine, rinse thoroughly, place in a large nonreactive pot, add the celery leaves and cook over medium heat for 4 to 5 hours or until corned beef is fork tender.

Serves 8-10.

Chuck Wagon Steak with Mushroom & Brandy Gravy

Billy the Kid probably ate more meals out-of-doors than indoors during his adult life. Some of the chuck wagon cooks were very resourceful. One can imagine one of the Chinese cooks, tired of preparing steak, steak, steak–picking some mushrooms and adding them to a steak while one of the hands contributed a little brandy from his private stock to the gravy.

1 1/2 pounds round steak, pounded to 1/4-inch thick
   or 4 good-sized cubed steaks

Cook the steaks in a cast iron skillet in a little butter or olive oil, then serve with **Mushroom and Brandy Gravy.**

Mushroom & Brandy Gravy

2 tablespoons butter
1/2 yellow onion, chopped
1 cup sliced white button mushrooms
1/2 cup dry white wine
1 1/2 cups beef stock or broth
1 1/2 tablespoons cornstarch
2 tablespoons brandy

Melt the butter in a saucepan, and sauté the onions and mushrooms until soft. Pour in wine, and 1/2 of the stock or broth and stir. Dissolve the cornstarch in the remaining 1/2 of the stock, stir into the sauce and cook, stirring constantly, until the gravy thickens. Remove the pan from the heat, stir in the brandy. Pour over the cooked steaks and serve.

Serves 4.

Cider-Basted Ham

The small tart apples of the New Mexico hill country make a wonderful cider and give this ham a unique flavor.

1 bone-in butt portion ham or 1/2 ham (about 7 pounds)
24 whole cloves
4 cups apple cider
2 white onions, peeled and cut into quarters
2 tablespoons brown sugar
2 tablespoons all-purpose flour
1 tablespoon lemon juice

Preheat oven to 350°. Rinse the ham in cold water, score the surface with a knife, making a diamond pattern on the top of the ham. Insert the cloves into the intersections of the cuts. Place the ham in a roasting pan. In a saucepan, bring the cider, brown sugar and onions to a boil, reduce the heat, cover and cook for 10 minutes. Strain off the onions and pour the cider over the ham. Bake for 2 hours, basting with the cider every half hour. Remove the ham from the pan and place the pan on top of the stove. Stir in the flour; add the lemon juice and simmer over low heat, stirring constantly, until the sauce has thickened. Slice the ham and serve with the sauce on the side.

Serves 8-10.

Two Sides to the Kid

Not many characters in the history of this country have gotten more attention, deserved or not, as Billy the Kid. His exploits have captured the imagination of Americans for the past century.

Was he a petty thief, who betrayed his friends, shot a man for every year he was alive and never did an honest day's work in his life? Or was he a frontier Robin Hood, who tried to work as a cow-hand and wound up on the wrong side of skirmishes over land disputes and fought against injustices of the day?

Coffee Roast Beef

This unusual way of preparing a beef roast was often used by cowboys and ranch hands while out on the range.

1 (3 1/2 to 4 pound) boneless rump roast
2 tablespoons cooking oil
1 yellow onion, cut into quarters
4 cloves garlic, cut in half
1 tablespoon tomato paste
2 cups medium strength black coffee
2 cups water
1 tablespoon butter
1/2 cup red wine

Preheat oven to 450°. Using a sharp knife make very small cuts in the roast and insert the garlic halves. Heat the oil in a heavy roasting pan or Dutch oven (cast iron works best) and sear the roast on all sides. Add the onion quarters, tomato paste, coffee and water to the pan and roast for 30 minutes. Reduce the heat to 375° and cook for 1 1/2 hours more or until the roast is done to taste. Remove the roast to a warm platter, let cool slightly and then slice. Stir the butter and wine into the pan juices and serve with the sliced roast.

Serves 8-10.

Billy Burger

1 pound lean ground beef
4 teaspoons blue cheese
Dashes of Worcestershire sauce

Divide the ground beef into fourths, then split each in half. Make each eighth into a patty. Sprinkle 1 teaspoon of blue cheese and a couple dashes of Worcestershire sauce on top of a patty. Top with another patty and seal the edges. Repeat the process with the balance of the meat then grill to taste.

Serves 4.

Beef Jerky

In the days Billy was roaming the New Mexico Territory, this was one of the best ways of preserving beef. It was also easy to carry when traveling by horseback. We don't know how many miles Billy the Kid traveled on horseback during his short lifetime, but we do know he covered a lot of sparsely populated territory. Beef jerky was a good way to stave off hunger pangs on those journeys.

Cut lean beef (round steak) into long, very thin strips approximately 1 1/2-inches wide. Rub the meat with coarse salt and hang in the sun to dry (or dry in a dehydrator.) If hanging outside, make a tent with cheesecloth to keep insects away from the meat. The meat should dry or cure in approximately two days. Make sure there is no moisture left in the meat before storing. The meat will be somewhat leathery when fully cured. Store in airtight containers.

Corn in a Kettle

1 tablespoon olive oil
1 clove garlic, minced
1 medium yellow onion, chopped
1 medium red bell pepper, seeded and chopped
1 tablespoon chopped fresh cilantro or parsley
1 can (16 oz.) hominy with the juice
2 cups fresh corn, cut off the cob, or frozen corn
1 mild long green chile, roasted, peeled, seeded and chopped
2 cups longhorn or colby cheese, shredded

Heat the oil in a frying pan, and sauté the garlic, onion and bell pepper until the vegetables are softened. Stir in the cilantro or parsley. In a casserole dish, layer the vegetables alternately with the hominy, corn and chopped chiles. Pour any remaining juice from the hominy over the top, then sprinkle with cheese. Bake in a 350° oven for 30 minutes or until cheese is melted and lightly browned.

Serves 6-8.

Barbecued Beef Brisket

1 beef brisket (8 to 10 pounds)
2 cans (12 oz. ea.) beer
1 tablespoon Worcestershire sauce
3 tablespoons dried, minced onions
2 cloves garlic, quartered
1 tablespoon chopped fresh parsley
Water

Trim any excess fat off the brisket and place it in a large roasting pan. Mix the beer, Worcestershire sauce, onions, garlic and parsley together, then pour over brisket. Add enough water to completely cover brisket. Cover with aluminum foil and bake in 275° oven for 8 to 10 hours or overnight until the brisket is tender. Let meat cool thoroughly, then slice, cover with **Brisket Barbecue Sauce** and reheat in a 350° oven.

Brisket Barbecue Sauce

1/4 cup olive oil
1 large yellow onion, chopped
2 cloves garlic, minced
1 tablespoon dry mustard
3 cups tomato sauce
1/2 cup red wine
1 1/2 cups water
1/4 cup lemon juice
1/4 cup Worcestershire sauce
2 tablespoons orange marmalade
1 teaspoon salt
1 teaspoon freshly ground black pepper
2 teaspoons chopped fresh parsley

Heat the oil in a large saucepan and sauté onion and garlic until onion is soft. Add the rest of the ingredients and simmer for about one hour. Store in the refrigerator until ready to use.

Twice Baked Chile Potatoes

3 large white baking potatoes
1 tablespoon olive oil
6 tablespoons butter, divided
1/4 cup yellow onion, minced
2 cloves garlic, minced
3 green chiles, roasted, peeled, seeded and chopped
Salt to taste
1 teaspoon freshly ground black pepper
1/4 cup milk
Parmesan cheese
Paprika

Preheat oven to 400°. Wash, scrub and dry the potatoes, coat lightly with oil. Bake for 1 hour or until the potatoes are done.

Heat 2 tablespoons of the butter in a frying pan, sauté onions and garlic until onions are soft. Add green chile, salt and pepper to the pan and cook, over low heat, until the chile is warmed through. Cut potatoes in half lengthwise and scoop out the pulp being careful not to cut through the skin of the potato. Mix potato pulp with the chile and onion mixture. Stir in the 4 remaining tablespoons of butter and the milk and spoon the pulp back into the potato shells.

Sprinkle with Parmesan cheese and paprika, return to the oven and heat, at 300° for 15 to 20 minutes or until the potatoes are warmed through.

Serves 6.

The Kinney Gang and Billy the Kid

A large cattle rustling operation took place just outside of Mesilla in a ranch owned by John Kinney. Jesse Evans, a friend of Billy's, was one of Kinney's men. The gang not only rustled cattle and horses but also robbed and even murdered when they felt it was necessary. After Billy left the Knight ranch in Burro Mountain he joined his friend Evans and rode with the gang. Although there is no official court mention of his adventures during these few months he was said to have taken part in many escapades including stealing cattle. Conveniently, the stolen beef were easily sold at Kinney's butcher shop in Mesilla.

Several writers have indicated that the period Billy the Kid spent with the Kinney gang was like a finishing school for gang members. In their company he honed his skills at breaking and, perhaps more importantly–avoiding the law.

New Mexico-Style Country Gravy

2 tablespoons sausage drippings or butter
2 tablespoons all-purpose flour
2 cups milk
1/2 tsp. freshly ground black pepper
Pinch of cayenne
Pinch of salt

Heat the drippings or butter in a cast iron skillet. Stir in the flour and lightly brown, about 2 minutes. Whisk in the milk, stirring constantly until the gravy is smooth. Add more milk if the gravy is too thick. Stir in the black pepper, cayenne, and salt. Serve hot over split ***Buttermilk Biscuits*** (see page 17).

Serves 4.

Cornbread Casserole

2 tablespoons olive oil
1 clove garlic, minced
1 large yellow onion, chopped
1 large green bell pepper, seeded and chopped
1 pound lean ground beef
1 long New Mexico green chile, roasted, peeled, seeded,
    and chopped
1 teaspoon salt
1/2 teaspoon ground black pepper
Dash of Tabasco®
1 can (17 oz.) whole kernel corn drained

Preheat oven to 400°. Sauté the garlic, onion and green bell pepper in the olive oil. Add the meat and brown. Stir in the other ingredients and simmer 15 minutes. Spoon into 9 x 13 casserole dish. Carefully pour **Cornbread Casserole Topping** over the meat mixture and bake for 30 to 40 minutes or until the casserole is bubbly and lightly browned on top.

Serves 6-8.

Cornbread Casserole Topping

1 egg
1/2 cup milk
1/2 cup stone ground cornmeal
1/2 cup all-purpose flour
2 teaspoons baking powder
1/2 teaspoon salt
2 tablespoons olive oil or melted butter

Put the egg and milk in a blender and blend until smooth. Add the rest of the ingredients and blend until just smooth. Do not overblend or it will be tough.

Marinated Catfish in Blue Cornmeal Batter

Marinade:
- 1/2 teaspoon ground oregano
- 3 tablespoons lime juice
- 3-4 green onions, chopped
- 3 tablespoons dry white wine
- 4 tablespoons olive oil
- 2 cloves garlic, minced

2 pounds catfish fillets
1 teaspoon pequin chile flakes
1/2 teaspoon salt
1/2 teaspoon ground black pepper
1 cup blue cornmeal
2 eggs, lightly beaten
2 tablespoons olive oil
2 tablespoons butter
Lime wedges

Mix the oregano, lime juice, onions, wine, oil, and garlic in a shallow glass dish. Arrange fish in the mixture and let marinate in the refrigerator for 45 minutes. Remove fillets from the marinade and discard the marinade.

Mix the chile flakes, salt and pepper with the cornmeal. Dip the fish in the beaten egg, then the cornmeal mixture. Heat the oil and butter in a frying pan, and sauté fish until golden brown. Serve with lime wedges.

Serves 4-6.

Trapper's Corn

This hearty dish was originally for the hungry men who worked and hunted in cold weather. Today, it makes a nice brunch entree anytime of the year.

1 pound pork sausage links
1 yellow onion, chopped
1 can (10 oz.) cream-style corn
1/2 teaspoon freshly ground black pepper
1/2 teaspoon salt
1 green chile, roasted, peeled, seeded and chopped
6 eggs
1 tablespoon white wine or water

Fry the sausage links until done, dry on paper toweling and then cut into bite-size pieces. Pour off all but approximately 3 tablespoons of fat from the frying pan, and sauté onions until lightly browned. Stir in the corn, pepper, salt and chile.

Beat eggs in a bowl with a wire whisk, add the wine or water and beat again. Stir eggs into the corn mixture, add the sausage pieces, scramble lightly and cook until eggs are set. Great served with hot buttered biscuits or flour tortillas.

Serves 6.

SOME SAY

Some say he was a bad man
Too handy with a gun.
Some say it was a terrible shame
That he spent his life on the run.

Some say he was the old West's
Version of a dashing Robin Hood.
Some say you shouldn't write
About him,
Others say you should.

"The Kid" in Lincoln County

'The Kid' first came to the attention of New Mexicans in the 'cattle war' of Lincoln County.

It was not only necessary that a cowboy should be an experienced *vaquero*, but also a good shot, and one who would fight for his employer. W.H. Bonney ('Billy the Kid') was a good horseman, an unerring shot and of reckless daring.

'The Kid' was employed by the Murphy Donlan faction, which he deserted and joined the John H. Tunstall-McSween faction. Bonney had killed Morton, Baker and 'Billy' Roberts. The sheriff of Lincoln County, Wm. Brady had a warrant for the arrest of Bonney and two associates. As Brady and his deputies, George Hindman and J.B. Mathews, were going to the courthouse in Lincoln, they were fired upon from ambush across the street by 'Billy the Kid,' Evans and Segura. The sheriff and Hindman were killed and 'the Kid' was slightly wounded by Mathews. 'The Kid' and his gang were then outlawed.

Cowcamp Cooking

CHAPTER FIVE

RANCH LIFE
AND THE
LINCOLN COUNTY WARS

When the eighteen-year-old Billy the Kid arrived in the bustling New Mexico town of Lincoln, he quickly found work with the Irishman, James. J. Dolan. Dolan was Major L.G. Murphy's business manager and they owned a bank and a mercantile business. The headquarters of L.G. Murphy and Company was housed in a two-story building which was the biggest facility in Lincoln.

The men who conducted their business from "The House," as it was called, were utterly ruthless and considered Lincoln County their personal fiefdom. Billy only lasted a few days working as a cowhand for Dolan before he had a run-in with Billy Morton, the hard-nosed foreman and was forced to move on.

He was quickly befriended by George and Frank Coe, who were cousins and had a small spread about ten miles south of Lincoln. He moved in with Frank Coe in the fall of 1877 before he started working for Tunstall on the Feliz and when the hostilities between the Murphy/Dolan and Tunstall/McSween factions erupted in the Lincoln County War, Frank Coe fought by the Kid's side.

Billy did a lot of hunting during that first winter in Lincoln. Since he was a crack shot he had no trouble bagging deer, turkeys, and an occasional bear so he and the Coes ate well. The Kid was said to be able to shoot a bear so far away no one else in the hunting party could even see it.

Stories handed down from people living in Lincoln at the time said that Billy was a pleasant looking, easygoing young man and although he was reported to already have killed several men he

(Continued on next page)

wasn't a grim man but had a ready laugh and loved to swap stories around a campfire.

Although he had very little formal education he was an avid newspaper reader, when he could find one. He was also well-spoken and did not make many glaring grammatical errors. He was never coarse and vulgar and rarely swore like most of the rough and tough men he rode with.

A free-spirited, generous man, he would help a friend anytime he was asked. Being a gambler he was either flush with winnings or dead broke after a bad run at the monte tables.

An article in the El Paso Herald, November 21, 1905 gives some insight in Billy the Kid's time spent in Lincoln and an account of the Lincoln County Wars.

EL PASO HERALD

El Paso, Texas   *November 21, 1905*

CAPITAN KILLING RECALLS EARLY FEUDS IN LINCOLN COUNTY; "BILLY THE KID"

Recent killing of Robert A. Hurt at Capitan, Lincoln County, New Mexico, as the alleged result of a feud, recalls to the minds of old-timers that Lincoln county has been the seat of many a feud, political, personal and otherwise, in days past.

At one time Lincoln county was the location of one of the hottest cattle feuds that ever existed in the west and more men were killed, it is declared, than in any feud that ever existed in New Mexico.

Pat F. Garrett, collector of customs at El Paso since 1902, when he was appointed by President Roosevelt, was the sheriff who broke up the feuds.

Garrett, though a quiet man, not given to boasting, often talked to his close friends . . . and others–of the days when he fought the cattle rustlers and the gunmen of Lincoln County and the stories, all substantiated by the court records of New Mexico, sounded like fiction, so bloody were many of the encounters.

Sheriff Pat Garrett

* * *

Rice, English Peas and Chorizo

There was a strong southern influence in New Mexico in both the cooking and the language. What Southerners call "English peas" are the same vegetable most Northerners or Yankees call "green peas."

1/2 pound chorizo*
1 tablespoon cooking oil
1 medium yellow onion, finely chopped
1 green bell pepper, seeded and chopped
1 cup uncooked white rice
1 cup hot water
1 can (10 oz.) tomatoes, with juice
1 cup chicken broth
2 tablespoons chopped fresh parsley
1/4 teaspoon freshly ground black pepper
1/2 teaspoon salt
1/2 teaspoon turmeric
1 cup frozen green (English) peas

Heat the oil in a large frying pan and sauté the chorizo until cooked through and lightly browned. Remove the chorizo from the pan, leaving the fat, and reserve. Sauté the onion and green pepper in the pan until soft. Add the rice; stir and cook until it starts to brown. Add the rest of the ingredients except the green peas and chorizo and cook, covered, until the liquid is absorbed. Then add the peas and chorizo and cook, over very low heat, until the peas and chorizo are warmed through.

Serves 4-6.

*Can be found in stores specializing in Southwestern/ Mexican food or see *Silver City Chorizo* (p. 42).

Eggplant Mexicano

5 slices bacon, chopped
1 onion, chopped
2 fresh tomatoes, chopped
2 jalapeños, seeded and chopped
1/2 cup chicken broth
1/2 cup dry white wine
1 teaspoon salt
1/2 teaspoon freshly ground black pepper
2 medium eggplants, peeled and cut into cubes
1 cup colby cheese, shredded

Preheat oven to 325°. Fry the bacon, remove from pan and reserve. Sauté onion in the bacon dripping. Add the tomatoes, jalapeños, chicken broth, wine, salt and pepper. Line the bottom of a glass casserole dish with half of the eggplant, spoon half of the tomato mixture over eggplant, sprinkle with half of the cheese and bacon. Repeat process ending with the cheese. Bake for 45 minutes, or until the eggplant is done and the cheese is melted and lightly browned.

Serves 4-6.

Devilish Potatoes

4 medium white potatoes, peeled, & thinly sliced
2 tablespoons olive oil
2 tablespoons butter
2 cloves garlic, minced
1/2 teaspoon pequin chile flakes
1/2 teaspoon dried rosemary, crushed
1/2 teaspoon salt
1/2 teaspoon freshly ground black pepper

Heat the oil and butter in a large frying pan, stir in the garlic, pequin chile, rosemary, salt and pepper. Then add the potatoes and sauté until golden brown.

Serves 4-6.

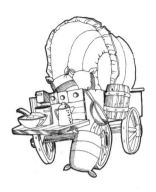

The Chuck Wagon Trail

In the mid-to-late 1800s cowboys could earn good money for a 14 to 16 hour day, busting ornery broncos, running some pretty mean cattle, sleeping on the ground, and performing their daily ablutions in the cold water of a creek.

They took turns singing softly to the cattle to keep them still, and guarding against rustlers. There was constant danger—they be could be thrown by a horse, trampled in a stampede or killed by a stray bullet.

So, although these men were paid well by the standards of the time, the one thing a cowhand wanted to know before signing on to an outfit was what kind of "chuck" was served. They knew they could stand all the other hardships if the food was good.

Unlike cowboys depicted in Hollywood movies these men called their food "chuck" and not "grub" which was the term used by miners. Motion pictures often depict the chuck wagon cooks as grizzled, crusty veterans of the bottle. Much closer to the truth was that the cook could be grouchy because he had to come up with great food under the worst possible conditions and most likely he didn't drink any harder than the rest of the crew. Very often a crew's cook was a cowboy who couldn't ride any longer due to an injury.

The kind of food served depended on what was available. However, the way it was prepared varied according to where the cook came from and who had influenced his style of cooking. In the New Mexico Territory the greatest influences were south-

(Continued on next page)

ern, Texan and Mexican. But every so often a Yankee dish would pop up on a menu–most likely a recipe learned from one of the homesteaders from New England.

Most chuck wagons were stocked with the basics: flour, pepper, salt, molasses, sugar, vinegar, some spices including cloves, cinnamon sticks, nutmeg, cayenne, chile powder, ginger and maybe some Mexican oregano.

Usually the chuck wagon was long on beef and short on vegetables and eggs, so the cook would try and trade a side of beef with a homesteader for whatever fresh supplies he could get.

Since beef was the basis for most of the trail meals, the cook had to be extremely inventive to come up with different ways to prepare it. Most often he cooked the beef over a grill or an open fire, frying it in a cast iron skillet. If the meat was overly tough, he'd boil it in a well-seasoned Dutch oven with vegetables or dumplings.

Photo courtesy Special collections, University of Arizona

Territorial Corn Pudding

4 eggs
2 cans (10 oz. ea.) cream-style corn
1 cup half-and-half
1/2 cup chopped cooked ham
2 tablespoons butter
1 clove garlic, minced
1/4 teaspoon cayenne
1/2 cup chopped green onions
**   (include tops)**
3 green chiles, roasted, peeled, seeded and chopped

Beat eggs, add the rest of the ingredients and pour into a well-greased 2-quart casserole dish. Cover with aluminum foil, make 5 to 6 holes in the foil to let the steam escape. Place the dish in a pan of hot water, making sure the water is only about halfway up the sides of the dish. Bake in a 350° oven for 45 minutes or until the mixture has set.

Serves 6-8.

Glazed Carrots & Onions

6 carrots, sliced
1 pound small onions (or quarter larger onions)
1/4 cup butter
2 tablespoons brown sugar
1/2 teaspoon ground ginger
1/2 teaspoon salt
1/2 teaspoon freshly ground black pepper
1/4 cup dark rum

Cook carrots and onions in a saucepan with water for 10 minutes or until tender. Drain, and return vegetables to saucepan. Add balance of ingredients and cook over medium-high heat, stirring frequently, until vegetables are glazed and just tender.

Serves 4-6.

Billy–Branded by Cain?

The journalists of the early twentieth century had a field day with Billy the Kid although their prose was often overly flowery and flamboyant and many of these reporters were not averse to doing a little preaching in their articles.

Here is an example from *The El Paso Herald,* August 29, 1901.

EL PASO HERALD

El Paso, Texas　　　　　　　　　　　*August 29, 1901*

It was in this land (Arizona), a land where law was still unknown, and where human life had not value, that Billy the Kid set up his own home, after that time when he first found the brand of Cain upon his brow. He fled, as the story goes, into old Mexico . . .

Now, by what inner workings of the human mind let us not seek to ask. Billy the Kid at once found himself past the point of all that consideration which usually enters into the plans of man-killing man. We may theorize or speculate as we like regarding the evolution of the bad man.

Scientists may tell us of degener-ates and that sort of thing today. At the time of Billy the Kid, the title of degenerate was not yet known. Had you asked any citizen of the far southwest why Billy the Kid was as he was, he would probably have told you that it was because he was born so.

He was not embittered by any early disappointments. He was never crossed in love, and, indeed, of love in its true form he was perhaps all his life in ignorance. He was an animal, pure and simple; an animal born with a cat soul, blood-thirsty, loving to kill. There you have it, and as to the reasons for it, let others answer.

Navajo Beans

1 pound pinto beans
2 large yellow onions, chopped
3 cloves garlic, minced
2 tablespoons olive oil

1 pound lean ground beef
1 cup tomato sauce
1 cup prepared salsa
1 teaspoon salt

Soak beans overnight. Pick out and discard the floaters and pebbles. Drain and discard the water. Cover with water again and cook for 2 hours or until tender. Sauté the onions and garlic in the olive oil, add the ground meat and cook over medium heat, stirring occasionally until the meat has browned. Stir in the tomato sauce and salsa and add to the beans with the liquid they cooked in. Simmer, over very low heat for 1 hour. Add the salt to taste.

Serve in bowls with **Navajo Fry Bread** (see p. 16) on the side to dip into the beans.

Serves 6-8.

Billy and San Patricio

Billy often visited San Patricio, the small community east of Lincoln. Billy especially liked to attend the many dances and parties held in the town. He was made to feel welcome at these festive occasions and was also often a favored guest in the homes of many eminent San Patricio families where they frequently invited him to dinners and parties. It was said that on those occasions his demeanor was decorous and his manner gentlemanly.

The ladies found him witty, charming and graceful. The older members of society were impressed with his youthful enthusiasm as well as his respectful nature.

San Elizario Rice

1 pound medium shrimp (20 to 25 count)
2 cups white rice
4 cups chicken broth
3 tablespoons butter
3 tablespoons olive oil
1 teaspoon red chile flakes
3/4 cup salted peanuts
1/2 cup green onions, finely chopped
2 cloves garlic, minced
1/2 teaspoon ground black pepper
1/4 teaspoon cayenne
1 tablespoon chopped fresh parsley
1 cup cooked ham, cut into cubes
chopped parsley for garnish

Devein shrimp and remove tails. Cook the rice in the chicken broth with butter for 20 minutes or until done. While the rice is cooking, heat the oil in a large frying pan, stir in the chile, peanuts, onions, garlic, pepper, cayenne, and parsley. Cook over medium heat for 2 to 3 minutes, stir in the ham and the shrimp and continue cooking until the shrimp are done, 5 to 7 minutes.

When the rice is done, toss with the shrimp and ham mixture, garnish with chopped parsley and serve.

Serves 6-8.

Noodle Cheese Ring

3 cups wide noodles
1 pint cottage cheese
1/2 pint sour cream
1 tablespoon melted butter

3 eggs, well beaten
1 teaspoon dill, chopped
1/2 teaspoon celery salt
1/4 teaspoon cayenne

Preheat oven to 325°. Cook the noodles according to package directions. In a small bowl mix the cottage cheese, sour cream, butter, eggs, dill, celery salt and cayenne together. Stir the sour cream mixture into the noodles and spoon into a well-greased ring mold. Place the mold in a pan of water, making sure the water doesn't come more than halfway up the sides of the mold. Bake for 1 hour. Unmold onto a platter, and serve warm.

Serves 4-6.

Zucchini Pancakes

3 cups zucchini, grated
1 teaspoon salt
1 teaspoon ground nutmeg
2 eggs, lightly beaten
3 tablespoons all-purpose flour
1/4 cup Parmesan cheese, grated
1/2 teaspoon freshly ground black pepper
2 dashes Tabasco®
3 tablespoons olive oil
3 tablespoons butter

Mix all the ingredients together, except the butter and olive oil. Heat the oil and butter in a large frying pan, drop heaping tablespoons of the batter for each pancake in the pan and sauté the pancakes until lightly browned on both sides.

Yields approximately 1 dozen pancakes.

Fried Green Tomatoes with Red Tomato Chile Sauce

4 large green tomatoes, sliced
2 eggs, lightly beaten
1 cup cornmeal
3 tablespoons olive oil
2 tablespoons butter
4 tablespoons grated cheddar or longhorn cheese

Dip the green tomatoes in the beaten egg, then dip in the cornmeal. Fry in the olive oil and butter until golden brown.

Place the fried tomatoes on a serving plate or platter, pour the **Red Tomato Chile Sauce** over them, sprinkle with the grated cheese and serve.

Serves 4-6.

Red Tomato Chile Sauce

1 cup chopped ripe, red tomatoes
1/2 yellow onion, chopped
1 clove garlic, minced
1 green chile, roasted, peeled, seeded and chopped
1 tablespoon chopped fresh parsley
1 teaspoon salt
1/2 teaspoon ground black pepper

Mix the chopped red tomatoes, onion, garlic, chile, parsley, salt and pepper together and warm in a saucepan or in the microwave.

CHAPTER SIX

GETTING CAUGHT
& DOING TIME
IN NEW MEXICO

The following newspaper account of the capture of the Kid and his trip, under guard, to Santa Fe gives not only an overview of this event but also provides us with an insight into the attitudes of the day towards the infamous outlaw.

THE LAS VEGAS DAILY OPTIC

Las Vegas, New Mexico   *Monday, December 27, 1880*

A BIG HAUL !
Billy Kid, Dave Radabaugh,
Billy Wilson and Tom
Pickett in the clutches of the law.
A Notorious Gang of Outlaws
Broken up, and the
Country Breathes Easier.

Our readers are familiar with the depredations committed in the lower country by a gang of daring desperadoes, under the leadership of Billy Kid, and of the repeated and unsuccessful attempts to capture them. They have roamed over the country at will, placing no value upon human life, and appropriating the property of ranchmen and travellers without stint. Posses of men have been in hot pursuit of them for weeks, but they succeeded in eluding their pursuers every time. However, the right boys started out, well mounted and heavily armed, and were successful in bagging their game.

YESTERDAY AFTERNOON the town was thrown into a fever of excitement by an announcement that the "Kid" and other members of his gang of outlaws had been captured, and were nearing the city. The rumor was soon verified by the appearance in town of a squad of men led by Pat Garrett, deputy sheriff of Lincoln county, and Frank Stewart, of the Panhandle country, having in custody the Kid, Dave Radabaugh, Billy Wilson and Tom Pickett. They were taken at once to jail, and locked up, and arrangements made to guard the jail against any attempt to take the prisoners out and hang them.

(Continued next page)

Feeling was particularly strong against Radabaugh who was an accessory to the murder of the Mexican jailor in an attempt to release Webb some months ago.

THE PURSUIT OF THE GANG

It will be remembered that Frank Stewart, with a party of picked men, left Las Vegas on December 14th to join Pat Garrett and his squad who were in waiting at Fort Sumner. The boys made a quick trip of it, arriving at the designated place of meeting on the night of the 17th instant. Nothing unusual transpired until the following night, when Kid's party approached the place, for the purpose of cleaning out Garrett's squad, not knowing that re-enforcements had come. Precaution had been taken to place a guard on the outside of the house, and upon hearing

THE CLATTER OF HORSES' HOOFS

in the distance, he warned his companions of the danger and they at once prepared to give the outlaws a warm reception. The night was very dark and foggy and even moving objects could be seen only at a very short distance. The first rider who came in range of the trusty Winchesters was Tom Follard who fell dead from his horse under the unerring aim of a half-dozen frontiersmen. Tom Pickett was following immediately behind, but after the first volley, he turned his horse and

FLED FOR HIS LIFE

Pursuit was out of the question, owning to the intense darkness that prevailed and the additional fact that a heavy snowstorm had set in. Dave Radabaugh's horse was shot but succeeded in carrying his rider a distance of twelve miles before dropping dead.

THE PARTY OF PLUCKY PURSUERS

now laid over two days starting forward on the evening of the third day, the 23rd. Promptly at the hour of twelve, they mounted their horses and rode twelve miles, to Wilcox's ranch. Here it was obtained that Kid and his followers had taken supper there the night before and were at their rendezvous, a vacant stone house, about three miles farther on. After a few moments' half the brave pursuers, for such they proved themselves to be, put spurs to their horses and rode quietly to the house designated as the hiding place of Kid's men. Upon approaching the premises, at 2 o'clock in the morning, three horses were seen hitched to the front door ready to be mounted

AT A SECOND'S NOTICE.

Garrett and Stewart at once surrounded the house, giving their men instructions to lay flat in the snow and await further developments.

JUST AT DAYBREAK

on the morning of the 24th a man supposed to be the Kid, but afterwards proving to be Charles Bowdre, appeared at the door. His body was pierced by two balls almost in an instant. The signal for shooting was given immediately upon the appearance of Bowdre, as Kid, who is a sure shot, had often boasted that he would never be taken alive. The only way to capture him, was to shoot him down at sight. The killing of Bowdre

(Continued next page)

alarmed those upon the inside of the house and they endeavored to ascertain what party was in pursuit of them; however, their calling elicited no response.

Two of the three horses standing at the door were

SHOT DOWN IN THEIR TRACKS

and the third one was shot in the doorway while Kid was in the act of getting the animal upon the inside out of the reach of the deadly bullets. The carcass of the dead horse across the threshold prevented Kid from leaping upon his horse, which was in the room with him, and attempting to escape. About four o'clock in the afternoon, the surrounded party

DISPLAYED A FLAG

and Radabaugh walked out boldly and said that they were willing to surrender, provided they were guaranteed protection. This was promised them and, in turn, "Kid," Billy Wilson and Tom Pickett joined Radabaugh upon the outside and gave themselves up to their captors, who put their prisoners on horses, doubling up as occasion required, and rode back to Wilcox's ranch, from which place a wagon was sent back after the young arsenal left at the robbers' rendezvous. The captors and their prisoners remained at the ranch all night, starting for Las Vegas on Christmas morning and arriving here before supper last night–very rapid riding. The party of men

WHO RISKED THEIR LIVES

in the attempt to rid the country of this bloodthirsty gang of robbers and murderers are deserving of un-

bounded praise and should be rewarded handsomely for their services. They will undoubtedly obtain the reward of $500 offered by the Governor for the capture of Kid, and it remains for interested citizens to raise a purse of money and present it to these sixteen men, as they have paid out money and endured hardships in the endeavor to hunt down and bring to justice one of the most desperate gangs of outlaws that ever terrorized the southwest.

THE PRISONERS

Kid is almost 24 years of age, and has an odd and pleasant cast of countenance. When interviewed between the bars of the jail this morning, he was in a talkative mood, but said that anything he might say would not be believed by the people. He laughed heartily when informed that the papers of the Territory had built him up a reputation second only to that of Victorio. Kid claims never to have had a large number of men with him, and that the few who were with him when captured were employed on a ranch. This is his statement and is given for what it is worth.

DAVE RADABAUGH

looks and dresses about the same as when in Las Vegas, apparently not having made any raids upon clothing stores. His face is weather-beaten from long exposure. This is the only noticeable difference. Radabaugh inquired somewhat anxiously in regard to the feeling in the community and was told that it was very strong against him. He remarked that the papers had all published exaggerated reports of the depredations of Kid's

(Continued next page)

party in the lower country. It was not half so bad as has been reported.

TOM PICKETT

Tom, who was once a policeman in West Las Vegas, greeted everybody with a hearty grip of the hand and seemed reasonably anxious to undergo an examination. Pickett is well connected, but has led a wild career. His father lives in Decatur, Wise County, Texas, and has served as a member of the Legislature. All the home property was once mortgaged to keep Pickett out of prison, but he unfeelingly skipped the country, betraying the confidence of his own mother.

BILLY WILSON

the other occupant of the cell, reclined leisurely on some blankets in the corner of the apartment and his meditations were not disturbed by our Farber pusher.

GREATHOUSE IMPLICATED

There remains no doubt of the fact that James Greathouse was a member of Kid's marauding party. Letters written by him to the talented rascal were intercepted in the mails. At one time he furnished horses for the Kid and his followers to escape from his ranch and, while in Las Vegas, wrote to the Kid warning him to leave the country or he would be captured. While in town he dispatched a courier to Bell's ranch for a horse, which he undoubtedly obtained and rode home on.

OFF FOR SANTA FE

Billy Kid, Billy Wilson and Dave Radabaugh, under the escort of Pat Garrett, Frank Steward, Mr. Cosgrove and one or two others, were taken to Santa Fe this afternoon. As the train was ready to leave the depot, an unsuccessful attempt was made by Sheriff Romero to secure Radabaugh and return him to the county jail. The engineer of the outgoing train was covered, by guns, and ordered not to move his engine. If the sheriff had been as plucky as some of the citizens who urged him forward, the matter would have been settled without any excitement whatever. The prisoner, Radabaugh, the only one wanted, was virtually in the hands of the United States authorities, having been arrested by deputy United States marshals, and they were in duty bound to deliver him to the authorities in Santa Fe. The sheriff and a few picked, trusty men, might have gone over to Santa Fe with the party, and, after Radabaugh's delivery, brought him back to Las Vegas, where he is badly wanted, not only by the Mexicans, but by all Americans who desire to see the law vindicated.

* * *

Irish Whiskey Cake

Being of Irish descent I'm sure that Billy's mother, Catherine Antrim, made many dishes from recipes the family brought with them from Ireland. This is a very distinctive cake that made a hit at special occasions.

2 cups sugar	3 1/2 cups all-purpose flour
1 cup butter	3 teaspoons baking powder
4 eggs	1/4 teaspoon salt
1 cup milk	1/4 cup Irish whiskey

Preheat oven to 325°. Cream the sugar and butter together. Lightly beat the eggs, and stir into the sugar mixture. Add milk and stir. Sift flour, baking powder and salt and add to the mixture. Stir in whiskey and beat very well. The secret to making this cake is to beat the batter a long time. Pour the batter in a greased and lightly floured bundt pan and bake for one hour, or until the cake tests done with a toothpick. Let cool on a wire rack and glaze with ***Irish Whiskey Glaze.***

Irish Whiskey Glaze

1 cup sugar	pinch salt
1 cup brown sugar	1/4 cup Irish whiskey
1/4 cup water	

Combine the two sugars, water and salt in a saucepan and bring to a boil. Cook until the sugars are completely dissolved. Remove from the heat, stir in the whiskey and drizzle over the cake while the glaze is still warm.

THE LAS VEGAS DAILY OPTIC

Las Vegas, New Mexico   *December 31, 1880*

"Acting Governor Ritch, in the absence of Governor Wallace, did not feel authorized to pay the reward of five hundred dollars offered by the Territory for the apprehension of Billy Kid; however, the citizens of Santa Fe raised that amount and gave it to Garrett and Stewart, accepting their order for the money."

Pumpkin Pudding

One can imagine Billy's mother making this treat. Pumpkins grew easily in most parts of the New Mexico Territory, and housewives in the nineteenth century were always experimenting with different ways to serve them. As a change in holiday fare, try this pudding for dessert with your Thanksgiving dinner.

2 cups mashed pumpkin
3/4 cup brown sugar
1/2 cup chopped pecans
1 teaspoon ground cinnamon
1/2 teaspoon ground nutmeg
1/2 teaspoon ground mace
1/2 teaspoon ground ginger
1/4 teaspoon ground cloves
1/4 teaspoon salt
3 eggs
1 cup whipping cream
3/4 cup milk

Preheat oven to 350°. Mix together the first nine ingredients. Stir very well. Beat eggs lightly and add to the mixture. Stir whipping cream and milk into the mixture and pour into a lightly greased glass baking dish. Place the dish in a shallow pan of hot water, making sure the water does not come more than halfway up the sides of the dish. Bake for one hour. Cool for 15 minutes and serve with whipped cream.

Serves 6-8.

Fruit Turnovers

This was supposedly one of the Kid's favorite desserts. He could stuff these in a saddlebag and eat them whenever his famous sweet tooth dictated. They are a simple straight-ahead no-nonsense dessert—a little like the Kid was himself.

Enough of your favorite pie crust for 2 nine-inch pies
1 cup mincemeat
1 cup apricot preserves
Brandy
Powdered sugar

Preheat oven to 375°. Cut the pie crust into 3-inch circles. Mix a splash of brandy with both the mincemeat and apricot preserves. Put 1 tablespoon of one of the fillings onto the top of each circle, fold over in half and crimp the semicircle edges together with the tines of a fork.

Prick the tops of the turnovers with a fork and bake about 20 minutes or until golden brown. Sprinkle with powdered sugar and serve hot or cold. These are excellent served with a scoop of vanilla ice cream.

Yields 12 turnovers.

Flan

Billy had a penchant for the ladies, especially Mexican señoritas. And women loved him. They were always trying to mother him—darning his socks or mending a torn shirt. And they loved to cook for him, too.

We can easily imagine one of the pretty señoritas, knowing how much Billy liked desserts, making this flan for him.

1 cup brown sugar
4 eggs
1/2 cup sugar
1/4 teaspoon salt
2 teaspoons vanilla
3 cups milk

Preheat oven to 350°. Divide the brown sugar equally in four custard cups. Put the cups in a large pan that has enough water to come halfway up the side of the cups. Bring the water to a boil. When the sugar has melted and turned a golden brown color, take a pair of kitchen tongs and tilt each cup until the caramelized sugar coats the inside of the cup about halfway up. Remove the cups from the water and let them cool.

Beat the eggs, then stir in the sugar, salt and vanilla. Scald the milk and slowly stir it into the mixture. Pour into the custard cups. Again place the custard cups in a pan that has enough water to come halfway up the sides of the cups. Bake for 1 1/2 hours or until done. Let cool before serving.

Serves 4.

Peach Cobbler with Brandy Sauce

2 cans (29 oz. each) sliced peaches
1 teaspoon cornstarch
1 cup sugar
2 tablespoons butter
1 teaspoon grated nutmeg
1 teaspoon ground cinnamon
1/2 teaspoon salt
1/2 teaspoon grated orange peel
1/2 cup brandy
3/4 cup slivered almonds
Pie crust

Preheat oven to 350°. Drain the peaches and reserve juice in a saucepan. Stir the cornstarch into the juice until dissolved. Add sugar, butter, nutmeg, cinnamon, salt and orange peel. Cook over low heat until thickened slightly. Remove from heat and stir in brandy. Arrange peaches in a 9 x 13 metal baking pan. Sprinkle almonds over peaches, and pour the sauce over the top. Cover with your favorite pie crust. Prick the crust with the tines of a fork and bake in 350° oven until slightly brown on top.

Serves 6-8.

Spanish Cream

2 envelopes unflavored gelatin
4 cups milk
1/2 cup sugar
3 egg yolks, beaten

3 egg whites, stiffly beaten
1 teaspoon vanilla
1/2 teaspoon almond extract

Sprinkle gelatin over milk, and cook over low heat. Beat the sugar and egg whites into the milk mixture, stirring constantly, until the mixture comes to a boil. Remove from heat and let cool. Stir in egg whites, vanilla, and almond extract. Spoon the mixture into individual molds, and place in refrigerator to set. Serve with sliced strawberries or peaches.

Serves 4-6.

Pastel Limón

(Lemon Pie)

1 tablespoon vegetable oil
2 tablespoons all-purpose flour
1 cup brown sugar
1 cup milk
2 egg yolks, lightly beaten
juice of one lemon
1 tablespoon grated lemon peel
1/2 teaspoon baking powder
2 egg whites, stiffly beaten
Deep dish prepared pie crust

Preheat oven to 425°. Mix all the ingredients together. Pour into the prepared pie crust. Bake at 425° for 10 minutes, then reduce heat to 350° and continue baking for about 45 minutes. Let cool, then refrigerate until ready to serve. Serve topped with fresh strawberries or raspberries.

Stovetop Rice Pudding

This pudding is from a by-gone era. It is what the trend setters now call "comfort food." And it is comforting to sit down in front of a roaring fire, with a cup of tea or a glass of whatever— and a bowl of this pudding.

2 cups water
1 cup white rice
1 tablespoon butter
Pinch salt
1/2 cup sugar
1 cup evaporated milk

2 teaspoons vanilla
1 teaspoon ground cinnamon
1 teaspoon ground nutmeg
1/2 cup raisins
Grated orange peel

Combine water, rice, butter and salt in a saucepan, cover and cook about 20 minutes or until rice is tender. Add the rest of the ingredients, except orange peel, and continue to cook, over very low heat, until thoroughly heated. (Do not let boil!) Sprinkle with a dash of grated orange peel before serving.

Serves 6.

Mesilla Valley Pecan Pie

3 eggs
2 cups light corn syrup
2 tablespoons all-purpose flour
1/4 teaspoon salt
2 teaspoons vanilla
2 tablespoons melted butter
1 tablespoon bourbon
1 cup pecan halves
1 unbaked 9-inch pie shell

Preheat oven to 425°. Beat the eggs well, and then stir in corn syrup, flour, salt, vanilla, melted butter and bourbon. Sprinkle the pecans in the bottom of an unbaked pie shell and pour the mixture over them. Bake at 425° for 10 minutes, reduce heat to 325° and bake for 45 minutes more or until the pie is firm in the center.

Peaches with Whiskey

I'm not sure that Billy and his friends would have cotton'd to the notion of pouring good whiskey over fruit and might have had some choice words for anyone who did–"dandy" being the most complimentary. Nevertheless, this is very good–especially as dessert after a heavy meal.

1 cup sugar
1 cup water

4 large ripe peaches
1/4 cup bourbon

Boil sugar and water together in a saucepan for 10 minutes. Peel, pit and slice peaches and poach them in the syrup until just tender. Remove from heat, stir in bourbon and let chill for at least 3 hours in the refrigerator. Drain, and serve in individual dessert dishes topped with whipped cream laced with brandy.

Serves 4-6.

Honey Raisin Bars

A Mesilla resident will tell you that some of the best honey in the world is produced in the Mesilla Valley. An old wives' tale has it that if you ate honey made from the pollen of something you were allergic to–such as alfalfa–you could cure the allergy. I don't know about that–but I know you can sure cure a sweet tooth with these cookies.

3 eggs
1/3 cup butter
1 cup honey
1/2 cup milk
3 1/2 cups all-purpose flour
2 teaspoons baking powder
1/2 teaspoon baking soda
1/2 teaspoon salt
1 teaspoon ground cinnamon
1/2 teaspoon ground nutmeg
1 cup raisins

Preheat oven to 375°. Beat eggs. Stir in honey and butter. Add milk, flour, baking powder, baking soda, salt, cinnamon, nutmeg and raisins. Mix together and spoon into a lightly greased 9 x 13 baking pan. Bake for 30 minutes or until done. Let cool and cut into bars.

Yields approximately 1 dozen bars.

THE LAS VEGAS DAILY OPTIC

Las Vegas, NM   *Tuesday, May 3, 1881*

LINCOLN, N.M. April 28– The notorious Lincoln county "Kid" is at large again! Late on last evening and while Deputy Marshal Olinger was at supper just across the road from the courthouse where Kid was confined, he heard three shots fired in rapid succession. Jumping up he ran across to the courthouse, opened the door to go upstairs and was met with a discharge of buckshot from a shotgun in the hands of the Kid. Just as his hand was on the door to open it, Old Man Goss called to him that Kid had killed Deputy Marshal Bell. Before replying the door was opened, he received the shot and fell backward exclaiming "Me too."

It is surmised that Kid snatched Bell's pistol while the latter was off his guard. At any rate Bell is dead, and Olinger is dead, both victims of Kid's wile and martyrs to their duties as peace officers in Lincoln county.

Sheriff Garrett was in White Oaks at the time collecting the taxes.

It will need coolness and bravery to recapture Kid. But if he remains in the United States it will be done.

After killing Bell and Olinger Kid compelled Mr. Goss to saddle Mr. Wm. Burt's horse for him, and rode quietly and leisurely out of town, no one offering to molest him in any way. The pusillanimity of such conduct by a whole town, and that town the county seat, is almost incredible. Yet such is the fact. Mr. Lilly, the keeper of the restaurant opposite of the courthouse, got down his gun and would have fired on Kid but was deterred by two men who were with him. Mr. J.H. LaRue got his gun down and was going to fire but was prevented by his wife. The balance of the population whether friends or enemies to the Kid, manifested no disposition to molest him.

Pat Garrett, with Mr. Goodleft, a former deputy in Colfax county, leaves today to stride Kid's trail. He says he will follow him to the end. Bell's body will be brought here for burial. Bob Olinger will be buried at Fort Stanton.

* * *

Carrot Cake

1 1/4 cups vegetable oil
2 cups sugar
3 eggs
1 small can crushed pineapple
2 cups shredded carrots
1 cup chopped pecans
1 cup coconut
1/2 cup raisins
2 cups all-purpose flour
2 teaspoons baking powder
2 teaspoons baking soda
1 teaspoon salt
2 teaspoons ground cinnamon
2 teaspoons vanilla

Cream oil, sugar and eggs well. Add pineapple, shredded carrots, nuts, coconut and raisins and mix well. Sift flour, baking powder, soda, salt and cinnamon together. Add to creamed mixture. Add vanilla last. Beat well and pour batter into a 9 x 13 cake pan. Bake 45 minutes at 350°. When done, cool and frost with *Carrot Cake Icing.*

Carrot Cake Icing

2 tablespoons butter, at room temperature
1 1/2 cups powdered sugar
1 teaspoon grated orange peel
1/2 teaspoon ground mace
1/4 cup drained, crushed pineapple

Beat together the butter and sugar until smooth. Stir in the rest of the ingredients until incorporated.

Molasses Bread Pudding

The housewives of the 1800s often had molasses for sweetening desserts when sugar was not available. Nothing went to waste in this era and bread pudding was a common way to use leftover bread.

2 1/2 cups dry white bread, broken into pieces
2 1/2 cups milk
2 eggs
2 tablespoons sugar
1/2 teaspoon ground cinnamon
1/2 teaspoon ground nutmeg
1 teaspoon grated orange peel
1/2 cup raisins
1/4 cup molasses
1 teaspoon vanilla

Preheat oven to 350°. Place the bread in a large bowl and pour the milk over it. Lightly beat the eggs, then stir in the sugar, cinnamon, nutmeg, orange peel, raisins, molasses and vanilla. Stir into the bread and milk mixture. Spoon into a lightly greased baking dish. Bake for 45 minutes or until the pudding tests done.

Serves 6-8.

Now You
See It . . .
Now You Don't!

One gentleman told the story, most likely apocryphal, that when he was young he and Billy the Kid sashayed into a saloon in what is now the old town of Albuquerque. Both men were about eighteen at the time. Although the saloon was crowded there wasn't enough excitement for Billy so he started firing his pistol into the ceiling. He made certain, however, that no one else actually saw him do it.

The bartender summoned a deputy sheriff. Both the bartender and the sheriff were convinced that the Kid was the culprit. But, when the deputy went to arrest him, Billy pointed out the fact that his gun holster was empty and argued that if he wasn't carrying a gun how could he have done the shooting?

The sheriff had to let the Kid go, although he and his companion were asked to leave the saloon.

Once they were on the street again, the Kid began to laugh. He then tipped his hat to show his friend that his gun was neatly resting in the hair on top of his head.

Christmas
Nut & Fruit Balls

Christmas traditions in New Mexico are unique. Traditional church services and Christmas trees are combined with such unique customs as the Posada, a procession from house-to-house on Christmas Eve that simulates the progress of Joseph and Mary as they went from door-to-door trying to find shelter on the night of Christ's birth.

At each house the members of the posada are invited in for refreshments. This is just one of the many goodies that might be offered.

1 cup figs
1 cup raisins
1 cup dried apricots
1 cup chopped walnuts
1 tablespoon dark rum or brandy
1 teaspoon grated orange peel
1/2 cup grated coconut

Process all the ingredients except the coconut in a food processor fitted with a steel blade. Shape the mixture into small balls. Put the coconut in a plastic bag and shake a few balls at a time in the bag until they are covered with the coconut. Store in the refrigerator until ready to serve.

Yields approximately 2 dozen.

THE LAS VEGAS MORNING GAZETTE

Las Vegas, New Mexico   Tuesday, January 4, 1881

A BRAG MARE

Everyone who has heard of Billy the Kid has heard of his beautiful bay mare, about whose speed some remarkable stories are told. Billy kept the beautiful mare very carefully and always reserved her for an emergency, fully appreciating her good qualities, and knowing full well that no other animal could run her down. There is no doubt in the minds of those who are most competent to judge but what she is the best animal in New Mexico. She was purchased from Texas stockmen a few years ago and wherever put to the test has demonstrated the fact that she was a remarkable piece of horseflesh. When Billy was besieged in the old stone house at Stinking Springs by the Stewart/Garrett party, he intended to make a break for liberty on her back Mazoppa-like, and expected that her fleetness would carry him out of harm's reach and from the bullets of the "dead shots" who were lying in wait for him. But the doorway being blocked by the body of a dead horse he was hemmed in. When he was finally rounded up, he presented the mare to Frank Stewart, knowing that he would appreciate her as he certainly did. Frank afterwards rode her in triumph to Las Vegas.

Those who have seen her have grown enthusiastic and it will be gratifying to our horsemen to know that the mare will remain in our neighborhood. W. Scott Moore, proprietor of The Adobe at the Hot Springs, made Frank Stewart a New Year's present of an elegant revolver valued at $60.00. One of many gifts our citizens have presented the brave Stewart as a testimonial of their appreciation of this good work in the campaign against the Kid's band. Not to be outdone, Stewart in turn presented to Mrs. Moore one of the best, if not *the* best animal in the territory.

* * *

Quince Preserves

1 pound quince, peeled
    and halved
1 1/4 pounds sugar

2 cups water
1 tablespoon grated
    orange peel

Cook all the ingredients in a saucepan over low heat until the fruit is tender. Remove quince with a slotted spoon, dice and put into sterilized jars. Bring the sugar syrup to a boil and then pour over the fruit. Seal, let cool and refrigerate.

Yields 4 half-pint jelly jars.

Grandma's
Molasses-Banana Bread

1/2 cup butter, at room temperature
1 egg, lightly beaten
1 cup molasses
3 bananas, mashed
1 3/4 cups all-purpose flour
2 teaspoons baking soda
1/2 teaspoon salt
1/2 cup chopped walnuts
1/2 teaspoon grated orange peel
1/2 teaspoon ground nutmeg

Preheat oven to 350°. Mix all the ingredients together, pour into 2 lightly greased and floured 5 x 9 loaf pans. Bake for 1 hour or until bread tests done. Let cool on a wire rack.

Yields 2 loaves.

Apple-Bourbon Pie

8-10 tart green apples
3 tablespoons all-purpose flour
1/2 teaspoon salt
1 teaspoon ground cinnamon
1 cup sugar
1 teaspoon vanilla

1 tablespoon bourbon
1 tablespoon lemon juice
3 tablespoons butter
2 (9-inch) pie crusts
1 egg, lightly beaten

Preheat oven to 425°. Peel, core and slice the apples. Place in one of the pie crust shells.

Mix together the flour, salt, cinnamon and sugar and sprinkle over the apple slices. Mix the vanilla, bourbon and lemon juice together and pour over the apple slices. Dot with the butter and cover with the top crust. Prick several holes in the top crust with the tines of a fork. Brush with the beaten egg and bake in a 425° oven for 10 minutes. Reduce the heat to 350° and bake for 45 minutes more or until top crust is nicely browned.

Applesauce Cake

1/4 cup butter
2 cups sugar
2 eggs
2 1/2 cups all-purpose flour
2 teaspoons baking soda
1 teaspoon salt
1 teaspoon ground cinnamon
1/2 teaspoon ground nutmeg
1/4 teaspoon ground allspice
1 1/2 cups *Homemade Applesauce* (see below)
1/2 cup raisins
1/2 cup chopped pecans

Preheat oven to 350°. Cream butter and sugar together. Lightly beat the eggs and add to the sugar mixture. Mix dry ingredients together and stir into the mixture. Add **Homemade Applesauce,** raisins and nuts and stir well. Pour into a well-greased 9 x 13 baking pan and bake for 45 minutes or until the cake tests done.

Homemade Applesauce

In Billy the Kid's day, they didn't run to the store to buy applesauce, they made it at home. It's easy to do and tastes better.

12 medium tart apples
Water
1 tablespoon lemon juice

1/2 cup sugar
1 tablespoon grated orange peel
1/2 teaspoon salt

Wash, peel and core apples. Coarsely chop apples and place in a large nonreactive saucepan. Barely cover apples with cold water, add lemon juice, and bring to a boil. Cover and cook over low heat about 45 minutes or until the apples are tender. Add sugar, orange peel and salt and stir well. Cook for another 5 minutes. Let mixture cool and then mash or blend in a blender. Store in the refrigerator until ready to use or serve.

Yields approximately 3 cups.

EPILOGUE

THE STORY ENDS, THE LEGEND BEGINS!

THE EL PASO HERALD

El Paso, Texas   *November 21, 1905*

After his escape from the jail at Lincoln ... Billy was next heard of at Las Tablas, where he had stolen a horse from Andy Richardson. He rode the animal within a few miles of Fort Sumner, when it broke loose and Billy walked into town.

He stole a horse from Montgomery Bell, which he rode away bareback. For some time he stayed with a sheep herder on Pete Maxwell's ranch, 35 miles east of Fort Sumner.

STAYS NEAR HIS CRIMES

This fugitive life lasted about two and a half months–hovering all the time around the scenes of his crimes of the previous two years.

'There seems to be a fascination, or an impelling power, which directs a criminal to the scenes of his crimes, notwithstanding the danger,' said Garrett in relating the story. 'He was an outlaw, under the sentence of death, and yet he lingered under the shadow of the gallows. He had many friends, and others aided him through fear.'

Upon being informed of the tragedy, Sheriff Garrett hastened back, and with deputies Tip McKinney and Joe Poe took up the trail of 'the Kid,' which led to his death.

Garrett had learned of Billy's movements, and he was expected to visit the house of Pete Maxwell. The house has long since been torn down and on the site is only a rough quadrangle of crumbling earthen walls. Speaking of this last scene in the tragic life of the most famous desperado of the southwest, Garrett described how 'the Kid' was killed.

KILLING OF THE KID

'The sheriff slipped into the Maxwell place and awaited the coming of Bonney at night. Pete Maxwell's bed was in one corner of the room, and I was sitting in the dark talking to Pete, who was in bed,' Garrett said, 'Bonney passed Joe Poe and Tip McKinney, my deputies, on what was then the gallery and came through the door. He could not tell who I was. "Pete," he whispered, "who is it?" He had his pistol, a double action 41 or A1? in his hand, and he motioned towards me with it as he spoke, still not recognizing me.

That was about all there was to it. I supposed he would shoot me and I leaned over to the left so that he would hit me in the right side and not kill me instantly, so that I could kill him, too.

I was was just a shade too quick for him. His pistol went off as he fell, but I don't suppose he ever knew who killed him or how he was killed.'

Mockingbird Cocktail

1 1/2 ounces tequila
1 ounce peach nectar
Juice of 1/2 lime

Club soda
Lime twist

Pour the tequila, peach nectar and lime juice over ice cubes in a highball glass. Add club soda to the top of the glass, and serve garnished with a twist of lime. Serves 1.

Earthquake Cocktail

1 ounce bourbon
1 ounce gin
1 ounce apple brandy

Stir together with ice, strain and serve in a stemmed cocktail glass. Serves 1.

The Cowgirl Cocktail

1/2 ounce brandy
1/2 ounce creme de cassis

1/2 ounce heavy cream

Shake with crushed ice and strain into a stemmed cocktail glass or serve over ice cubes in a lowball glass. Serves 1.

The Fallen Angel Cocktail

2 ounces gin
Juice of 1 lime
Dash bitters

1/2 teaspoon white
creme de menthe

Stir well with ice and strain into a stemmed cocktail glass. Serves 1.

Spiked Tea

1 cup strong cold green tea
1/2 cup rum
1/4 cup brandy

2 teaspoons sugar
Lemon slices

Mix all the ingredients together and pour over ice in highball glass. Garnish with lemon slices and serve. Serves 1.

Lady Luck Cocktail

2 ounces gin
1/2 ounce lime juice

1/2 ounce grapefruit juice
2 teaspoons sugar

Put all the ingredients in a blender with crushed ice, strain and serve in a cocktail glass. Serves 1.

Horse's Neck

• 2 ounces bourbon or rye   • 1 lemon   • Ginger ale

Peel the lemon in one long spiral piece and place peel in a tall highball glass, draping one end over the edge of the glass. Fill glass with ice cubes, pour bourbon over ice, fill with ginger ale and serve. Serves 1.

Frutas con Vino
(Fruit & Wine Punch)

2 cups fresh strawberries
4 medium ripe peaches
1/2 cup sugar

2 bottles (750 ml. each)
sparkling white wine
ginger ale or citrus soda

Hull and slice the strawberries. Peel the peaches, pit and slice. Lightly toss both the strawberries and peaches with the sugar. Add 1 bottle of the wine, and chill for 8-10 hours. Chill the remaining bottle of wine and add just before serving along with ginger ale or citrus flavored soda to taste. Makes approximately 24 (1/2 oz.) cups punch.

Gee-Haw Cocktail

This cocktail was said to be popular at the more posh hotels in Santa Fe in the latter part of the nineteenth century. I once asked for this drink at a Santa Fe landmark hotel, but the bartender just shook his head and asked me if I'd order something simple.

2 1/2 ounces gin
1 ounce dry vermouth

1 ounce grenadine
3 drops of bitters

Shake well with crushed ice and strain into a stemmed cocktail glass. Serves 1.

Index

(continued next page)

(continued next page)

(continued next page)

Index (continued from previous page)

Meet the Author

Lynn Nusom has owned and operated award-winning restaurants and was the executive chef of a four-star four-diamond hotel. He writes a newspaper column on food, reviews cook books, writes magazine articles on cooking and makes frequent appearances on television demonstrating cooking techniques.

Lynn Nusom has written a wide variety of cook books including; *Cooking in the Land of Enchantment, Spoon Desserts; Custards, Cremes and Elegant Fruit Desserts, Christmas in Arizona, Billy the Kid Cook Book, Christmas in New Mexico, New Mexico Cook Book, The Tequila Cook Book* and *The Sizzling Southwestern Cookbook.*

The author makes his home in southern New Mexico.

More Cook Books by Lynn Nusom

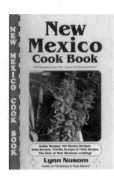

NEW MEXICO COOK BOOK

Authentic history and foods of New Mexico. Includes chapters on Indian heritage, chile as a way of life, Mesilla Valley, Santa Fe, Albuquerque, Taos & New Wave recipes. Try *Onion Pie, Sopaipillas, Navajo Corn Chowder, Hopi Scalloped Red Peppers & Corn, Chile Verde* and more!
5 1/2 x 8 1/2—144 pages . . . $6.95

THE TEQUILA COOK BOOK

Taste the spirit and flavor of the southwest! More than 150 recipes featuring tequila as an ingredient. Wonderful appetizers, soups, salads, main dishes, breads, desserts, and, of course, drinks. Includes fascinating tequila trivia. Truly a unique book and a great gift item!
5 1/2 x 8 1/2—128 pages . . . $7.95

CHRISTMAS IN NEW MEXICO COOK BOOK

Recipes, traditions and folklore for the Holiday Season—or all year long. Try *Three Kings Bread, Posole de Posada, Christmas Pumpkin Pie, Christmas Turkey with White Wine Basting Sauce*, and many more.
6 x 9—144 pages . . . $9.95

CHRISTMAS IN ARIZONA COOK BOOK

'Tis the season . . . celebrate Christmas in sunny Arizona. Read about the fascinating southwestern traditions and foods. Create a southwestern holiday spirit with this wonderful cookbook.
5 1/2 x 8 1/2—128 pages . . . $9.95

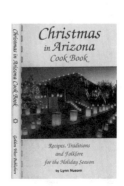

SALSA LOVERS COOK BOOK

More than 180 taste-tempting recipes for salsas that will make every meal a special event! Salsas for salads, appetizers, main dishes, and desserts! Put some salsa in your life! Over 360,000 in print. By Susan K. Bollin.

5 1/2 x 8 1/2 — 128 pages . . . $6.95

REAL NEW MEXICO CHILE
The Insider's Guide to Cooking with Chile

Delicious, creative New Mexican dishes by Albuquerque food columnist Sandy Szwarc. Learn the secrets of cooking with chile, that distinctive ingredient of New Mexican cuisine!

5 1/2 x 8 1/2 — 112 pages . . . $6.95

ARIZONA TERRITORY COOK BOOK

Authentic recipes from Indians, Cowboys, The Military, Mexicans, Miners, and Mormons plus a healthy helping of history makes this a full meal! By Daphne Overstreet.

5 1/2 x 8 1/2 — 120 Pages . . . $6.95

COWBOY CARTOON COOKBOOK

Zesty western recipes, cowboy cartoons and anecdotes. Cowboy artist Jim Willoughby and his wife, Sue, combined their many talents to produce these palate-pleasing selections. Saddle up the stove, 'cause you'll be riding the range tonight! Yee-hah!

5 1/2 x 8 1/2 — 128 pages . . . $7.95

KOKOPELLI'S COOK BOOK

A fascinating collection of authentic Southwestern and American Indian recipes and over 50 hand-illustrated reproductions of Mimbres pottery. Includes mythology and historical trivia. By James and Carol Cunkle.

5 1/2 x 8 1/2 — 112 pages . . .$9.95

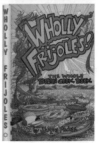

ORDER BLANK

GOLDEN WEST PUBLISHERS

☼ 4113 N. Longview Ave. • Phoenix, AZ 85014

www.goldenwestpublishers.com • **1-800-658-5830** • FAX 602-279-6901

Qty	Title	Price	Amount
	Arizona Cook Book	**6.95**	
	Arizona Territory Cook Book	**6.95**	
	Best Barbecue Recipes	**6.95**	
	Billy the Kid Cook Book	**7.95**	
	Chili-Lovers' Cook Book	**6.95**	
	Christmas in Arizona Cook Book	**9.95**	
	Christmas in New Mexico Cook Book	**9.95**	
	Cowboy Cartoon Cook Book	**7.95**	
	Grand Canyon Cook Book	**6.95**	
	Kokopelli's Cook Book	**9.95**	
	New Mexico Cook Book	**6.95**	
	Quick-n-Easy Mexican Recipes	**6.95**	
	Real New Mexico Chile	**6.95**	
	Salsa Lovers Cook Book	**6.95**	
	Take This Chile & Stuff It!	**6.95**	
	Tequila Cook Book	**7.95**	
	Texas Cook Book	**6.95**	
	Tortilla Lovers Cook Book	**6.95**	
	Western Breakfasts	**7.95**	
	Wholly Frijoles! The Whole Bean Cook Book	**6.95**	

Shipping & Handling Add: United States $3.00
Canada & Mexico $5.00—All others $12.00

☐ My Check or Money Order Enclosed   Total $ _____

☐ MasterCard ☐ VISA ($20 credit card minimum)   (Payable in U.S. funds)

Acct. No. _____ Exp. Date _____

Signature _____

Name _____ Phone _____

Address _____

City/State/Zip _____

Call for a FREE catalog of all of our titles

1/03   **This order blank may be photocopied**   Billy the Kid